Cambridge Ele

Cambridge Elements in Internat
edited by
Kenneth Reinert
George Mason University

DEBT SUSTAINABILITY

A Global Perspective

Ludger Schuknecht
Asian Infrastructure Investment Bank

CAMBRIDGE
UNIVERSITY PRESS

CAMBRIDGE
UNIVERSITY PRESS

University Printing House, Cambridge CB2 8BS, United Kingdom

One Liberty Plaza, 20th Floor, New York, NY 10006, USA

477 Williamstown Road, Port Melbourne, VIC 3207, Australia

314–321, 3rd Floor, Plot 3, Splendor Forum, Jasola District Centre,
New Delhi – 110025, India

103 Penang Road, #05–06/07, Visioncrest Commercial, Singapore 238467

Cambridge University Press is part of the University of Cambridge.

It furthers the University's mission by disseminating knowledge in the pursuit of
education, learning, and research at the highest international levels of excellence.

www.cambridge.org
Information on this title: www.cambridge.org/9781009218481
DOI: 10.1017/9781009218528

© Ludger Schuknecht 2022

First published 2022

A catalogue record for this publication is available from the British Library.

ISBN 978-1-009-21848-1 Paperback
ISSN 2753-9326 (online)
ISSN 2753-9318 (print)

Debt Sustainability

A Global Perspective

Cambridge Elements in International Economics

DOI: 10.1017/9781009218528
First published online: August 2022

Ludger Schuknecht
Asian Infrastructure Investment Bank

Author for correspondence: Ludger Schuknecht, mail@ludgerschuknecht.de
or ludger.schuknecht@aiib.org

Abstract: This Element presents the facts, arguments and scenarios around public debt from a global perspective. The largest economies especially feature record debt and fiscal risks, including from population ageing and financial imbalances. With low interest rates, there is no imminent problem. But at some point, debt will have to come down. There are four possible scenarios for how debt could come down. First, governments could economise and reform. Second, governments could default. Third, governments could erode the real value of debt via inflation and negative real interest rates. However, this scenario cannot continue forever. Policy errors can prompt a loss of confidence, destabilisation and crisis. This fourth scenario last included the largest economies in the 1970s. It would become a major global challenge if it were to happen again in today's interconnected world.

Keywords: private and public debt, debt sustainability, public expenditure, financial stability, debt scenarios

ISBNs: 9781009218481 (PB), 9781009218528 (OC)
ISSNs: 2753-9326 (online), 2753-9318 (print)

Contents

Real knowledge is to know the extent of one's ignorance.

He who will not economize will have to agonize.

(Confucius)

Executive Summary

The debate around public debt and fiscal risks is very controversial. Some claim that sustainability risks are already very high while others suggest that more debt could serve the 'common good'. This study presents the facts, arguments and scenarios for public debt dynamics in the future. It finds that a prudent approach is the best but perhaps not the most likely way forward.

Many countries feature record levels of public debt. This concerns especially the largest economies. Fiscal support programmes in the COVID-19 pandemic were necessary to protect incomes and economic capacities but they aggravated the debt situation. Further challenges amplify fiscal sustainability risks: high and unproductive public spending and the future costs of population ageing, low growth, high private debt and potential financial crises with international contagion. There are also questions over future inflation and real interest rates, the costs of decarbonisation and geopolitical conflicts. As long as a favourable financing environment prevails, there is no imminent problem. But at some point, risks will have to be dealt with and debt will have to come down.

Four possible scenarios describe how the reduction of excessive debt and vulnerabilities could unfold. First, countries could reform and consolidate to bring growth up and fiscal and financial imbalances down. This is likely to happen in many small economies but prospects are more uncertain in the larger ones. Second, countries could seek 'debt workouts' that imply a negotiated reduction in the real value of debt. Some small economies may find this a suitable option, despite the political costs that might arise.

Third, countries could engage in financial repression to reduce the real value of debt gradually via inflation and low interest rates. This is already happening and it may continue for a long time. However, this scenario is only stable if confidence is maintained and major policy errors and shocks are avoided. Once confidence drops, financial repression could mutate into destabilisation. This fourth scenario would be particularly troubling if it were to involve the largest economies.

Financial repression can build a bridge to consolidation and reform so that the destabilisation scenario is avoided. The adjustment effort needed is feasible and the return is considerable: maintaining confidence in public finances will keep our economies stable, reduce societal tensions and benefit the poor and middle classes the most. It will also allow us to master population ageing, decarbonisation requirements and geopolitical challenges.

1 Introduction

High debt and fiscal risks trap governments and reduce the policy space beyond fiscal policies more than we think. Over-indebted, we depend more and more on a continuing upswing which causes uncertainty, reduces confidence and at times even crises.

(Jacques de Larosière, 2019)

Fashion is not restricted to clothes, and when ideas become fashionable, they are just as resistant to objective criticism as the length of skirts. That is why all economic ideas need to be freely discussed and judged against the facts of real life.

(Prince Philip, Duke of Edinburgh)

Debt and finance have been amongst the most ingenious but also most controversial inventions of humanity. Debt has been financing business opportunities, wars or big festivities for millennia. Homer and Sylla (1991) in their fascinating history of interest rates report the first evidence on debt from about 5000 years BC. The Babylonians introduced the Code of Hammurabi, the first code for debtor–creditor relations, in about 1800 BC, specifying limits to interest rates and credit conditions. At that time, interest rates were very high by today's standards: 25–50% per annum for grain and metal. The Greeks and Romans introduced such codes following domestic debt crises and these codes were so well done that they were valid for centuries. Government debt appeared for the first time in the third and second centuries BC in the Greek City-States and the Roman Empire before taking off in the Middle Ages and modern times.

Throughout history, all genres of writing have discussed the ups and downs of debt, of government debt and private debt, of the relations between debtors and creditors, and the economic, distributional, social, moral and political questions revolving around it. Debt is the motive in many crime stories and real-world dramas.

The drama and divisiveness of optimism and credit booms ending in the tears of default have been known since the ancient Greeks (Homer and Sylla, 1991). It became a frequent phenomenon in modern times (Reinhart and Rogoff, 2009; Eichengreen et al., 2021). It is perhaps best embedded in the global public's memory through the Latin American crisis of the 1980s, the Asian crisis of the late 1990s, the repeated Argentinian defaults over recent decades and the European fiscal crisis with the Greek tragedy of 2009–2015 (Papaconstantinou, 2016). Debt is, therefore, one of the most dramatic embodiments of evolving human ingenuity and cooperation but also of excesses and tragedy.

1.1 Two Visions of Public Debt and Fiscal Risks

Public debt and fiscal risks have reached historical records at the global level and in many countries, and projections do not point to a decline. This is an indisputable fact, as we will see below. But whether this situation is concerning because of the implied sustainability risks and whether something needs to be done about it are subject to a very controversial debate.

Some economists argue that today's situation implies huge risks. Low interest rates have induced governments, corporations and households to take on ever more debt. The dynamics of debt is unsustainable. The quality of public and private debt is declining. Debt undermines growth prospects as low-return investments proliferate and unproductive zombie firms are kept alive. Future liabilities from population ageing, financial crisis, climate change and geopolitical challenges add to fiscal risks. When interest rates rise, many countries if not the world will be in big trouble.

Consolidation and reform are, therefore, needed sooner rather than later, and they should be underpinned by rules and institutions that constrain public spending and debt accumulation in the post-COVID world. This will preserve the solvency and well-functioning of our market economies and allow us to master the challenges of the future (Heinemann et al., 2018; Schuknecht et al., 2011).

Other economists argue that more debt is even a desirable development, especially in advanced countries. This includes many prominent economists, including Blanchard (2019) and Krugman (2020), and New Monetary Theorists like Kelton (2020). According to their assessment, there is too much saving in the world and governments need to make up for the lack of demand with higher public deficits and debt. If the money is well spent on public investment, the additional spending's positive growth effects finance the additional debt easily. Moreover, more spending will keep more people employed and, thus, prevent 'scarring' from the loss of human capital.

Fiscal consolidation to bring down debt 'too soon' will, therefore, be self-defeating as it will hurt growth and confidence. Proponents of this view acknowledge that there are limits to debt but they are regarded as being far away. Moreover, governments can and should fine-tune demand, and rules-based policies are too rigid. Only this will allow us to master the challenges of the future.

Who is right? The doom-mongers deploring soft budget constraints and weak incentives as the root of moral hazard and bankruptcy in the 'mother of all debt bubbles'? Or the idealists who confuse the aspiration of benevolent and omniscient governments willing to implement their smart policy advice with the reality of 'policy' makers being 'irresistibly attracted to public debt' (Tanzi, 2016 and 2018)? Both worlds are of course caricatures and a balanced assessment is required instead.

Indisputably, we need government with public spending financed by taxes to provide core public goods and services – the history of government over the past 150 years is in fact a huge success story in this regard (Schuknecht, 2020b). At the same time, politicians and bureaucrats are just human beings, prone to error and excesses, like everybody else. They need constraints on spending and deficits so that their action fosters a competitive, sustainable and socially balanced market economy instead of inviting rent-seeking and promoting crony capitalism (Erhard, 1957). Limitless spending and debt arguably do not make people happier while they breed waste and privilege. Politics need constraints especially in good times, so that debt accumulation in the inevitable bust is indeed followed by debt reduction, as Keynes requested.

1.2 Gauging the Need for Action

The ability of governments to respond strongly to crises has proven its value in the COVID-19 pandemic. Enormous public stimulus programmes replaced faltering private demand and mitigated supply shocks, thus protecting many jobs and firms. This benefitted people directly during the pandemic and it also preserved the economic structures that allow a swift recovery as the pandemic comes to an end.

However, the pandemic and earlier episodes of crisis and recession have left a legacy of debt, vulnerabilities and disincentives that need to be addressed at some point. At the same time, population ageing, financial instability, decarbonisation and geopolitics constitute major economic and fiscal policy challenges. The scope of imbalances is quite significant but not unmanageable. There are good reasons not to wait too long to move back onto solid ground.

This requires taking stock of the post-COVID situation, including the fiscal risks lying ahead. It also requires an analysis of the possible scenarios for debt reduction in the future so that we know what options we have and what their costs and benefits will be. This study will be international and global in scope. Along the way, there will be more emphasis on the highly indebted advanced countries. But the situation of emerging economies will also receive due attention, given their growing economic weight in an increasingly interconnected and interdependent world.

1.3 Debt-Related Risks Warrant Debate: Mapping the Study

Public debt is at record levels globally and in many economies, especially the largest ones. This coincides with large contingent liabilities emerging from population ageing and risks in the financial sector; add to that the future challenges of climate change and geopolitical conflicts. These are the facts discussed in Section 2. They have made many countries' public finances vulnerable to even moderate changes in interest rates, external shocks and policy errors.

There are further factors that may aggravate sustainability risks but not all of them receive the attention which they deserve. Section 3 argues that high public spending is not neutral and may itself become a risk driver, especially if it is unproductive and goes beyond what is financeable. Growth prospects may be lower than we think due to poor framework conditions, decarbonisation requirements, the zombification of our companies and growing protectionism. Asset price booms turning to bust and rising inflation and real interest rates would weigh on financing conditions, growth and public finances. These risks could be exacerbated by growing concerns about the credibility of the institutional frameworks that we erected for our economies, our currencies and public finances. International interdependence and open capital markets could speed up and exacerbate an eventual loss of confidence.

What are the choices for bringing debt down and what would they imply? Section 4 looks at four scenarios. The first scenario describes debt reduction via consolidation and structural reforms. Many countries have successfully taken this route. The section also discusses 'debt workouts' as a second scenario of orderly debt reduction. This is politically costly and seems more feasible for smaller than for large countries. Scenario 3 involves reducing the real value of debt via negative real interest rates. Such financial repression has worked to some extent and for a limited time in the past. It did so in a number of countries in the late 2010s and it is expected to continue doing so going forward.

But repression might get out of control and mutate into destabilisation when financing costs rise, and policy errors and external shocks occur. The section describes the possible evolution of this fourth scenario. It is a risk scenario, not the baseline, but such scenarios have happened many times before as well. In the 1970s, it involved the US and the UK, two of the largest economies at the time. The impact was huge, but it could well be stronger, faster and more contagious if it happened in today's global economy and affected its largest countries. However, financial repression might also build a bridge to consolidation and reform with more sustainability and resilience as the prize.

This Element does not provide an account of fatalistic and speculative doom-mongering. It describes the situation we are in, the risks we face, the choices we have and the scenarios they would lead us into. Chances are that major crises can be avoided. The risks and remedies are well known and the magnitude of reform is feasible.

At the same time, the political economy and the zeitgeist do not favour determined action and even point in the other direction. Still, the risks are there and, from an encompassing, global perspective, they may be larger than we perceive. Reinhart and Rogoff (2009) asked why countries did not act preventively before crisis struck. Many times, people have believed, or wanted to believe, that 'this time is different'. And yet, 'the universe loves nothing so much as to change the things that are and to make new things like them', as the Roman emperor Marcus Aurelius said almost 2,000 years ago.

2 Public Debt and Sustainability

> The superior man, when resting in safety, does not forget that danger may come. When in a state of security, he does not forget the possibility of ruin. When all is orderly, he does not forget that disorder may come. Thus, his person is not endangered, and his States and all their clans are preserved.
>
> (Confucius)

> If you do not know history, you think short term. If you know history, you think medium and long term.
>
> (Lee Kuan Yew, 1998)

2.1 Introduction

Public debt is a Janus-headed 'invention' (James, 2021). It allows governments to do many productive and necessary things that otherwise would have to wait. But there would also have been fewer wars and 'white elephants' if there had not been the possibility to make future generations pay for them. And when there has been too much debt, the ensuing crises have never been pleasant.

Public debt has affected the course of history (Eichengreen et al., 2021). North and Weingast (1989) argue that the rise of the UK and the USA as leading global powers was closely linked to their credibility in repaying public debt. It allowed the two countries to borrow more and more predictably than their competitors because they would not default. Hence, it helped them to become world leaders. The two World Wars also left winners and losers very highly indebted, and the strong economic and financial muscle helped the Allied Forces to win. In the global financial crisis and the COVID-19 pandemic, rising debt helped prevent financial and health disasters turning into economic and social disasters.

Nobody questions the need for incurring debt in the midst of a crisis but the main challenge arises afterwards. On most occasions in history, countries paid up – the USA, the UK and France have never defaulted in the past 200 years. Sometimes the debt was simply too high though. Some countries openly and repeatedly defaulted. Others did not default but inflated their debt away – slowly or suddenly – when the debt burden became economically or politically too high. This happened time and again in history (Reinhart and Rogoff, 2009). The hyperinflations in Germany of 1923 and in twenty-first-century Zimbabwe are probably amongst the best-known examples in a long history of (slow or fast) default via inflation.

This is not today's situation and it is not our prospect. But in order not to get there, it is important to understand and acknowledge the challenge – which is the aim of this section.

2.1.1 The Merits of Sound Public Finances

Given the controversial discussion over the merits and demerits of public debt, it is worth recalling why sound public finances with high-quality spending and sustainable debt are so important in modern economies. First, they are a prerequisite for the sound functioning of government itself. Only with sufficient financial means can governments conduct fiscal policies towards the production of essential goods and services in an orderly manner. Financial problems cause ad hoc disturbances and 'stop-and-go' policies that are detrimental to people's trust in government. They tend to hurt the most vulnerable people in society who depend on good government services. High-quality spending and sustainable debt also ensure that we can master the fiscal challenges of the future, from population ageing to climate change. Sound public finances are hence deeply social and the strong correlation between trust in government and low debt in Europe is no surprise (König and Schuknecht, 2019).

Second, sound public finances are also important for the functioning of the economy per se. They allow the private sector sufficient room for its activities and provide the necessary stability for investment and innovation. They ensure that central banks can preserve trust in money via price and financial stability so that citizens and companies have a credible and reliable store of value, medium of exchange and unit of account.

Third, sound public finances are also essential for the proper functioning of financial markets, which serve as the 'lubricant' of the economy. Government debt provides a liquidity and funding buffer for banks and non-bank financial institutions. Banks hold large amounts of government debt on their balance sheets that could get them into financial trouble, should their government experience financing difficulties.

Finally, sound public finances also ensure confidence in the currency of a country. Fiscal crises produce contagion, disrupt international stability and undermine the international standing of a country. This is particularly relevant given that debt is very high at the global level and in most large countries. International spillovers and spillbacks could be very large and unpredictable.

2.2 A Recent History of Public Debt

In 2020/21, public debt was very high by any historical standards in many countries and notably in the largest ones. Advanced country public debt stood at about 120% of GDP in 2020 (Figure 1; see also IMF 2021a, IMF definition of 39 advanced economies). The G7 countries even featured more than 140% of GDP on average (Table 1). These debt figures are very similar to those prevailing in 1946, directly after World War II, except that they were reached during times of peace and not war.

On the IMF's metric of public debt, Japan topped the 'league' at some 256% of GDP in 2020. Italy was second at almost 156% of GDP followed by the United States (133%). France, the United Kingdom and Canada (three other G7 countries) plus Spain, Belgium and Portugal fell into the 100–130% range in 2020. Germany was an outlier of sorts with 'only' 73% of GDP and many smaller countries still saw debt near or below 60% (Annex Table).

Emerging economies featured much smaller public debt ratios. The average in 2020 was about 64% and slightly higher in Asia at 68% (Table 2). Hence the magnitude of emerging economy debt in the early 2020s is comparable to advanced countries in the 1990s. Still, differences across countries are huge and some of the largest countries are also highly indebted. Public debt in Brazil and Argentina was around the 100% of GDP mark in 2020. China's public debt was on average near 67% of GDP (though there are significant potential further liabilities; see Wong, 2021) while India reported almost 90% of GDP.

There are good reasons for debt increases in crisis times such as the two World Wars, the global financial crisis or the COVID-19 pandemic. In the pandemic, the magnitude of stimuli in advanced countries was staggering: over 15% of GDP of additional spending and forgone revenue and over 10% of GDP in loans, equity or guarantees (Figure 2). Figures were much smaller but still substantial in emerging economies and developing countries. As a result, public deficits shot up from almost −3% in 2019 to −11.7% in advanced countries and from −4.7 to −9.8% in emerging economies.

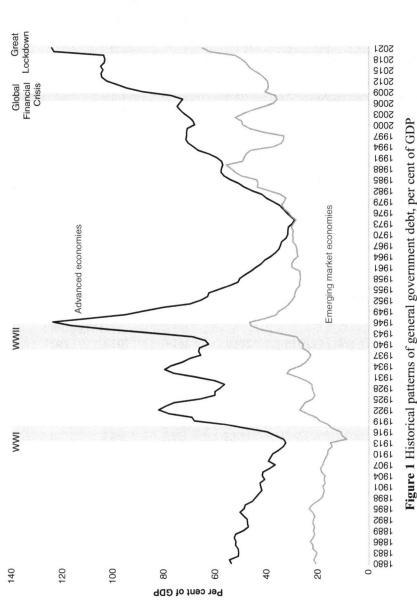

Figure 1 Historical patterns of general government debt, per cent of GDP

Sources: IMF, Historical Public Debt database; IMF, World Economic Outlook database; Maddison Database Project; IMF staff calculations

Note: The aggregate public-debt-to-GDP series for advanced economies and emerging market economies is based on a constant sample of twenty-five and twenty-seven countries respectively, weighted by GDP in purchasing power parity terms.

Table 1 General government gross debt and overall balance

	Gross debt (per cent of GDP)			Overall balance (per cent of GDP)	
	2007	**2019**	**2020**	**2021**	**2020**	**2021**
G7	84.4	118.0	136.7	139.5	−13.2	−11.9
Canada	65.0	86.8	117.8	116.3	−10.7	−7.8
France	63.8	98.1	113.5	115.2	−9.9	−7.2
Germany	65.0	59.6	68.9	70.3	−4.2	−5.5
Ireland	24.9	57.4	59.8	63.2	−5.3	−5.5
Italy	103.4	134.6	155.6	157.1	−9.5	−8.8
Japan	187.7	234.9	256.2	256.5	−12.6	−9.4
Spain	36.1	95.5	117.1	118.4	−11.5	−9.0
Switzerland	43.6	39.8	42.9	44.8	−2.6	−3.4
United Kingdom	44.1	85.2	103.7	107.1	−13.4	−11.8
United States	62.1	108.2	127.1	132.8	−15.8	−15.0

Source: IMF

Table 2a General government debt, 2016–26, per cent of GDP

			Projections	
Gross debt (per cent of GDP)	**2016**	**2019**	**2020**	**2021**
World	83.2	83.7	97.3	98.9
Advanced Economies	105.5	103.8	120.1	122.5
Emerging Market Economies	48.4	54.7	64.4	65.1
Asia	**50.0**	**57.3**	**67.6**	**69.9**
China	48.2	57.1	66.8	69.6
India	68.7	73.9	89.6	86.6
Indonesia	28.0	30.6	36.6	41.4
Malaysia	55.8	57.2	67.5	67.0
Philippines	37.3	37.0	47.1	51.9
Singapore	106.5	129.0	128.4	129.5
Thailand	41.7	41.0	49.6	55.9
Russian Federation	14.8	13.8	19.3	18.1
Latin America	**56.4**	**68.4**	**77.7**	**75.9**
Argentina	53.1	90.2	103.0	
Brazil[2]	78.3	87.7	98.9	98.4
Mexico	56.7	53.3	60.6	60.5
South Africa	51.5	62.2	77.1	80.8

Source: IMF

Table 2b General government fiscal balance, 2016–21: overall balance, per cent of GDP

			Projections	
	2016	**2019**	**2020**	**2021**
World	−3.5	−3.6	−10.8	−9.2
Advanced Economies	−2.7	−2.9	−11.7	−10.4
Emerging Market Economies	−4.8	−4.7	−9.8	−7.7
Asia	−4.0	−5.9	−10.8	−9.2
China	−3.7	−6.3	−11.4	−9.6
India	−7.1	−7.4	−12.3	−10.0
Russian Federation	−3.7	1.9		
Latin America	−6.0	−4.0	−8.8	−5.7
Argentina	−6.7	−4.5	−8.9	
Brazil	−9.0	−5.9	−13.4	−8.3

Source: IMF

Note: All country averages are weighted by nominal GDP converted to US dollars (adjusted by purchasing power parity only for world output).

2.2.1 Debt Dynamics over Recent Decades

Historically, debt has been a seesaw. In prosperous peace times, debt always came down – during the long period of growth and stability before World War I, the intermittent growth spurts of the 1920s and late 1930s and the post–WWII recovery between 1945 and 1975. This was for good reasons: good times were followed by bad times and countries only 'survived' crises if they had taken preventive action before. The experience of countries that did not manage was a deterrence to the others.

This 'consensus' broke down in the 1970s. Debt rose gradually from about 30% of GDP to 60% on average in the advanced countries in the late 1970s and 1980s. After that, it increased in three waves back to post–WWII ratios: the recession of the early 1990s (plus 10 percentage points), the global financial crisis (plus 30 percentage points) and the COVID-19 pandemic (plus 20 percentage points). The G7 allowed the debt ratio to increase from about 82% to 141% of GDP in just thirteen years (Table 1). By contrast, there were also several small to mid-sized countries that kept public debt quite low and below the 'famous' 60% of GDP threshold in the European Union (see Section 2.3 and the Annex Table). Emerging economies experienced more moderate dynamics and managed to bring debt down during recovery periods (Figure 1).

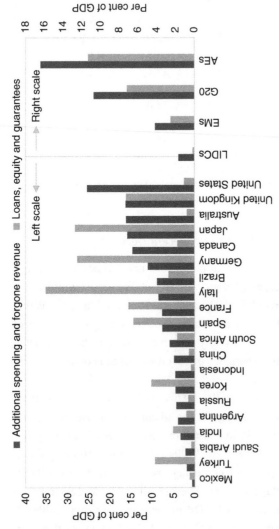

Figure 2 Government fiscal support in response to COVID-19, 2020–1, percentage of 2020 GDP

Source: IMF (2021a)

Note: Country groups include low-income developing countries (LIDCS), emerging economies (EMs), the G20 countries and advanced economies (AEs).

Given the upward trending debt in many advanced countries, is our way of running public finances like 'war in slow motion'? Or has something fundamentally changed so that the 'old laws' do not apply any longer – 'is this time truly different?'

2.3 Limits to Sustainable Debt

2.3.1 'Safe' Debt Thresholds

There are no absolute truths on 'safe' versus 'unsafe' levels of public debt. What is safe depends on many things: fiscal deficits, expenditure quality and the tax potential, economic growth and growth prospects, the development and stability of financial markets and other factors. Up until the mid-2000s, perhaps even the mid-2010s, there was a broad consensus that high debt undermined growth and raised government financing costs. Debt should, therefore, normally not exceed certain threshold values. Empirical studies saw such public debt thresholds at around 80–100% of GDP, depending on the country and the study (Reinhart and Rogoff, 2010; Checherita-Westphal et al., 2014).

With these arguments in mind and also considering the risk of moral hazard and free-riding if governments were fiscally unconstrained, European countries decided that the common European currency, the euro, should be underpinned by sound public finances in its member countries. The threshold for debt that countries were supposed to comply with over time was set at 60% of GDP. Any country with figures which were typical of the time (ca 5% nominal growth, 2% inflation and 5% interest rates) would then keep its debt ratio stable even if the deficit reached 3%. Perhaps equally significantly, 60% was broadly the debt ratio of France and Germany, the two most important players. The IMF in the 1990s broadly supported these thresholds in its analysis. Lower ratios were recommended for emerging and developing countries with low credibility, under-developed financial markets and a significant share of foreign financing.

In the 2010s, it became increasingly clear that the growth and interest assumptions underlying the 60% threshold did not hold any more. Economic growth had declined but interest rates had declined even more. On this basis, a serious debate emerged on whether even much higher benchmarks such as 100, 150 or even 250% of GDP should still be regarded as 'safe'. It was argued that growth-enhancing spending may lead to less debt in the long term if it exerts a strong positive effect on growth (IMF, 2021a).

The other reason for suggesting higher 'safe' public debt ratios relates to the demand for 'safe assets' in financial markets. The actors in the financial sector – banks, asset managers, life insurance companies – want to hold safe and liquid assets to avert problems in periods of market volatility with significant redemptions and this role can be played by (safe) government debt. Moreover, regulatory requirements favour the holding of government debt as it counts against liquidity and long-term funding requirements and as banks do not need to hold collateral against credit to governments. If there is a shortage of 'safe assets', more public debt is needed.

Counter-arguments point to the fact that the shortage is artificial. There will not be any shortage of 'safe assets' once central banks stop the purchase of government debt. On the contrary, some countries' debt may turn out to be too high to be considered safe by market participants once the market mechanism is working again. Less debt would then mean more 'safe assets' (Hartmann and Smets, 2018; Schuknecht, 2018).

There are obviously limits to public indebtedness and there are thresholds – 'tipping points' at which unfavourable dynamics may set in (Schuknecht, 2018; Brunnermeier, 2021). Nobody knows the precise magnitude of these thresholds, though, and they are likely to change across countries and over time. Still, some rule-of-thumb figures might be useful. The IMF presents a number of countries with private and public debt ratios near or above 240% of GDP as highly indebted. Most of these countries feature public debt of 100% of GDP or more; some feature particularly high private debt. The European Commission applies the Treaty's 60% threshold for (net) public debt and a private debt 'ceiling' of about 165% in its risk analysis.

These figures are much higher than the thresholds used in earlier decades. Still, one could view these numbers – total debt of near or above 240% of GDP with public debt of more than 60%–80% – as useful, though crude, benchmarks for advanced countries in the debate on safety thresholds. This is especially true when acknowledging the fiscal risks from population ageing and from private debt via the financial sector that almost all advanced and emerging countries will face in the future. Immigration might mitigate the costs of population ageing for some countries but hardly in all ageing economies, given the magnitude of the effect. Decarbonisation costs and geopolitical challenges may add to this. In the global financial crisis, some advanced countries got into difficulties even with much less public debt (see Section 2.4 below). Emerging economies remain well advised to orient themselves on more prudent thresholds.

2.3.2 Financing Debt

Interest rates and financing costs are key factors for the question of whether debt is considered to be high or even too high. In the short term, higher debt and rising interest rates can cause liquidity problems, especially when much debt needs to be refinanced. In the long term, they can drive a country into insolvency. In the 'real world', the distinction between the two concepts is somewhat artificial. Investors can become reluctant to finance a government in the short term (liquidity) owing to concerns about sustainability (solvency) in the long term.

In any case, higher interest payments crowd out other (productive) government spending, require higher (growth-reducing) taxes or simply lead to even more debt. Some European countries painfully experienced these trade-offs in the high-interest period of the 1980s and early 1990s. Italy, for example, spent a peak of 10% of GDP – over one-fifth of total spending – on debt service in the early 1990s (Tanzi and Schuknecht, 2000).

Paradoxically the situation in the early 2020s with much higher public debt seems to be comparatively 'harmless'. From a historical perspective, debt service costs for government have hardly ever been lower (Figure 3). In the 2010s, interest rates became widely negative in real terms and even negative in nominal terms for a number of countries in Europe. In many advanced countries, the interest rate became lower than the economic growth rate, which reduced sustainability risks.

Still, concerns remain. First, the favourable growth-interest differential does not benefit all countries and typically applies least to those economies with high debt. In Italy, the effective interest rates (which are the average rates the government actually paid) on government debt were almost always higher than economic growth (Figure 4; see also Fuest and Gros, 2019). Second, debt may not explode when growth is higher than the interest rate but, depending on the situation, it could rise to very high levels which may be economically and financially unsustainable. Japan's public debt, for example, had increased to 256% of GDP in 2020 because average deficits have been very high for decades. High domestic savings facilitate public debt financing

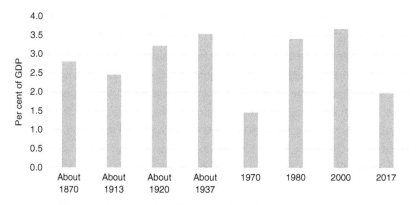

Figure 3 Interest spending on public debt, per cent of GDP
Source: Schuknecht (2020b)

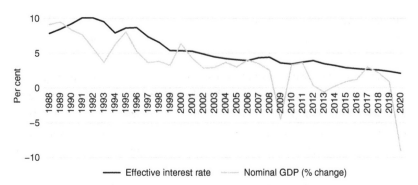

Figure 4 Italy: effective interest rate and nominal GDP growth
Source: IMF (2021f)
Note: Effective interest rate is the average rate the government paid on its debt in that year.

more than elsewhere. But if past patterns continue, debt will continue rising even further. It would ultimately raise the question where the limit for public debt is also in Japan.

A third reason for caution is the vulnerability of countries to interest rate increases when public debt is very high. Economists call it stress testing when they check how much the interest burden of government goes up when rates rise. Assume that countries need to finance about 20% of GDP every year and the interest rate rises by 3%. The interest burden then reacts very differently depending on the debt level (Figure 5). A country with 70% of GDP of public debt, roughly Germany in 2020, needs to pay 0.2% of GDP more interest on its debt within one year and 2.1% over time. This is not at all trivial. In 2015, 2.1% of GDP was almost half of Germany's education expenditure. But for a country with debt of 120% or 250% of GDP, the increase would be much more serious and would reach several per cent of GDP over time.

One could argue that the assumptions are unrealistic, interest rates do not rise that much and not all debt is turned around in five years. The assumptions are, nevertheless, reasonable to proxy situations of significant stress. Interest rates on public debt can rise significantly and fast. They increased by several per-centage points within a few weeks in the context of the European fiscal crisis that started in 2009 (see Section 3). Moreover, government borrowing require-ments in the EU in 2020 – new debt and maturing debt – were 25% of GDP, more than a quarter of total debt (Table 3) and they are projected to remain high. Hence, 20% of GDP is not a bad assumption for stress testing annual gross financing needs, especially for highly indebted countries.

Table 3 Gross financing needs, components, 2020 projections, per cent of GDP

	Budget deficit (per cent of GDP)	Maturing debt (per cent of GDP)	Stock flow adjustment (per cent of GDP)	Gross financing needs (per cent of GDP)
Austria	9.6	8.5	0.3	18.4
Belgium	11.2	13.5	1.2	26.0
Finland	7.6	9.1	1.2	18.0
France	10.5	15.8	0.2	26.5
Germany	6.0	12.4	3.7	22.0
Ireland	6.8	7.8	−2.1	12.4
Italy	10.8	20.7	1.3	32.7
Netherland	7.2	8.9	2.4	18.4
Spain	12.2	15.8	−0.2	27.8

Source: European Commission (2021)

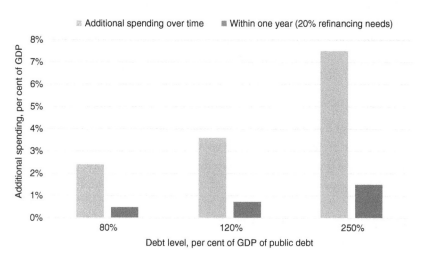

Figure 5 Stress test: additional spending with a 3% interest increase within one year and over time

Source: Own calculations

Moreover, and contrary to what one might expect, advanced countries have lengthened the maturity structure of their debt only a little, despite record low interest rates. Spain, Italy and the USA featured an average maturity of five-and-a-half to seven years and the UK almost fifteen years for their central government debt in late 2020/early 2021. This is mostly a modest increase compared with the beginning of the millennium. However, when taking into account central bank asset purchases, the effective maturity from an interest risk perspective has even fallen (see also Section 3.4).

The fiscal risks emanating from central bank asset purchases can be illustrated with the case of Japan: the Bank of Japan held 95% of GDP in central government bonds in late 2020. A 1% central bank interest rate increase would, under certain assumptions, cost the bank about 1% of GDP in profits within one year, which implies commensurately lower transfers to the government budget.

The assumption of higher interest rates and financing costs is also fully in line with EU long-term projections of about 4% nominal long-term interest rates (European Commission, 2021). The US Congressional Budget Office (CBO) sees higher rates (2.6% real by 2050) and higher debt service costs as the main reason for a potential public debt explosion in the next thirty years (Figure 6).

If we expect higher interest rates in the future, the process of reducing excessive debt needs to start well before. This is because, with moderate growth, it takes quite a long time to bring debt down even with a near-balanced budget (see Section 4.2). Germany took a decade to reduce public debt from a little over 80% to 60% of GDP before COVID-19 struck. For very highly indebted countries, it will be the task of a generation – just as it was after World War II.

2.4 Fiscal Risks from Population Ageing and Financial Crises

2.4.1 Population Ageing and Social Spending

There is another major and well-known fiscal challenge which puts sustainability at risk in the future: population ageing. This will affect most advanced and many emerging economies. In the most rapidly ageing countries, there may be fewer than two people employed for each person in retirement in a decade or two. If current social security systems are maintained, this will imply higher spending, especially on pensions, health and long-term care, which the young of today will need to finance.

The overall dynamics and magnitude of this challenge are enormous, even though there are significant differences between countries. In 1960, social spending as defined by the OECD stood at 'only' 9% of GDP or about one third of total government spending in advanced countries. By 2017, this share had increased almost threefold to 24% of GDP. Pensions (over 9% of GDP) and health spending (7% of GDP) were the most important components. Since 1980, every decade saw an increase in the spending ratio of about 2% of GDP. This happened when demographics were still relatively favourable because benefit levels and eligibility were extended enormously (Schuknecht and Zemanek, 2020).

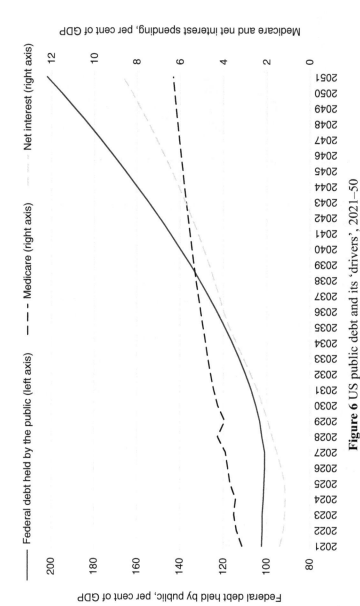

Figure 6 US public debt and its 'drivers', 2021–50

Source: United States, Congressional Budget Office (March 2021)

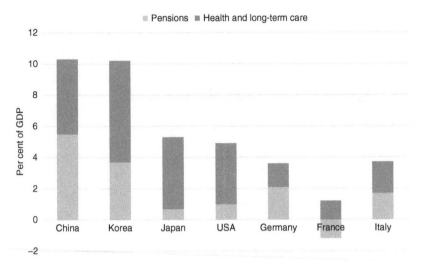

Figure 7 Projected increase in ageing-related spending, 2015–50
Sources: European Commission (2018); OECD; IMF

A simple extrapolation of these trends would bring social spending to about 30% of GDP by 2050, an increase of 6 percentage points of GDP. The European Commission (2017 and 2020/21) is more optimistic and assumes an increase in the order of 2.5% of GDP, and 4% of GDP in a risk scenario for the EU by 2050 (European Commission, 2021). Projections diverge significantly across countries (Figure 7). France expects no further increase in social spending in the coming decades, Germany projects almost 4%, and the USA and Japan would face around 5% of additional spending without further reforms. Projections for emerging economies are in some cases even higher. The EU Commission sees an increase of up to 10% of GDP in some European emerging countries and some projections for Korea and China are of a similar ballpark.

The projected spending increase of several per cent of GDP over the coming three decades in an environment of high deficits and public debt constitutes a huge fiscal risk. As mentioned, this corresponds to countries' public investment or even their education budget. In net-present-value terms, these fiscal obligations can reach several hundred per cent of GDP.

2.4.2 Private Debt and Financial Crises

More and more observers acknowledge that the debt increases that could arise from high private debt and risks in the financial sector are also hugely important. The sole focus on public debt used to be a serious omission from a comprehensive view of what level of debt is 'safe' or sustainable. Banking and financial crises linked to excessive private debt and asset price bubbles have historically been very costly to public budgets and resulted in major debt increases. In some countries, they have brought national governments to their (financial) knees.

Whether private debt is likely to impact on public finances depends on a number of factors. Normally, when households have difficulties servicing their mortgages and corporations their debt, the financial sector as intermediary absorbs related losses. But when losses are too great and the financial sector is weak, financial crisis can emerge. The government is then asked to step in and prevent a broader collapse in the financial system and, by implication, in the economy.

Before the global financial crisis, the costliest crises were in emerging economies. Gross fiscal costs had reached a staggering 30–50% of GDP in Indonesia, Chile and Korea in the 1980s and late 1990s (Table 4). With the global financial crisis, advanced countries experienced similar if not more dramatic crises with huge fiscal costs and debt increases (Figure 8). Spain and Portugal saw their debt ratios increase by over 60 percentage points of GDP which brought Spain to 100% of GDP and Portugal to 130% of GDP after the

Table 4 Financial crisis support before 2007

Country	Crisis dates	Total gross fiscal cost (per cent of GDP)
Average all	1970–2007	14.8
EU countries	1970–2007	6.6
Finland	1991–4	12.8
Norway	1991–3	2.7
Sweden	1991–4	3.6
Argentina	2001–5	9.6
Brazil	1994–6	13.2
Chile	1981–7	42.9
Indonesia	1997–2002	56.8
Japan	1997–2002	14.0
Korea	1997–2002	31.2
Mexico	1994–7	19.3
Malaysia	1997–2002	16.4
Russia	1998–2000	6.0
Thailand	1997–2002	43.8
Turkey	2000–3	32.0
Uruguay	2002–5	20.0

Sources: Laeven and Valencia (2008)

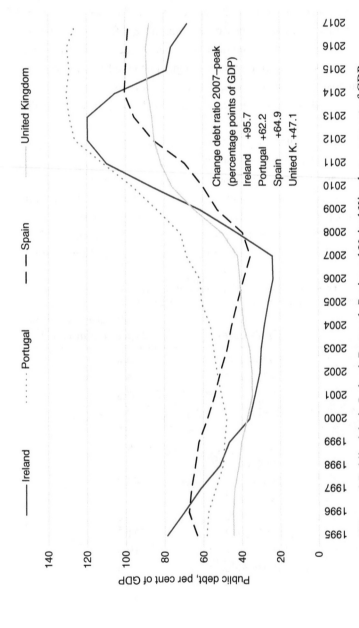

Figure 8 Public debt in Ireland, Portugal, Spain and United Kingdom, per cent of GDP

Sources: OECD; Schuknecht (2020b)

financial crisis. The most dramatic debt increase of almost 100 percentage points of GDP between 2007 and 2012 was experienced by Ireland where bank bailout costs alone exceeded 30% of GDP.

Nobody had expected such fiscal crises in advanced countries. Ireland and Spain experienced fiscal crisis despite very low debt levels at the outset – 20% and 35% of GDP – because their financial systems and economic competitiveness had become very weak. Linking this up with the earlier debate, safe debt levels hence depend very much on the overall circumstances and situation of countries. Borio et al. (2016 and 2020) and Schuknecht (2020b) emphasise the large fiscal costs of financial crisis and the need for very high safety margins. The European experience after the global financial crisis suggests that the Maastricht public debt limit of 60% of GDP is perhaps quite reasonable after all, so as to reduce the risk of a financial crisis turning into fiscal crisis.

Looking forward, regulatory reforms and capitalisation efforts have made banks much stronger today than before the global financial crisis. Therefore, related fiscal risks should also be lower. However, there are still risks of renewed financial sector turmoil for three reasons.

First, it is not only public debt but also private debt that reached new record highs in 2020 (Figure 9). Global public debt and corporate debt each exceeded

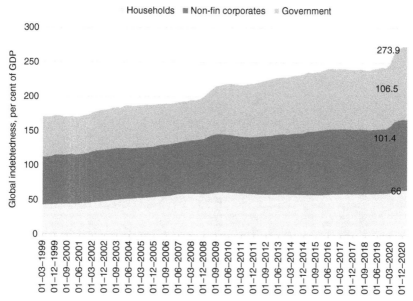

Figure 9 Global indebtedness by sector, 1999–2021, per cent of GDP
Source: IIF (2021a)

100% of GDP, which was significantly higher than before the global financial crisis. Household debt had also increased, though less strongly, to a new record of 66% of GDP. Looking at individual countries, a number of large countries feature total indebtedness of near or above 240% of GDP, the benchmark mentioned above. Debt was by far the highest in Japan at around 400% of GDP (Figure 10). France and Canada followed with around 300% of GDP. Other countries with very high private debt included Korea, Australia and China.

Historically, high asset prices and low rates and risk premia on debt have contributed to the private sector debt build-up and risk-taking, as many observers have lamented (IMF 2021c). If these extraordinary conditions reverse, financial crisis with severe fiscal costs can arise from recapitalising financial institutions and adverse economic effects.

Second, there are significant implicit liabilities in the financial sector through the holdings of government debt in the financial system. The magnitudes of government debt in the hands of the financial sector are enormous. In several European high-debt countries, they reached 20–30% of GDP in the hand of banks plus another 20–30% of GDP in the hands of the non-bank financial sector. Banks are especially vulnerable when their capital is threatened by a revaluation of their government debt holdings. This happened, for example, in the context of the Greek debt restructuring in 2012 and again in 2015.

Third, guarantees have become an important contingent liability for many governments with the COVID-19 crisis. Governments issued guarantees to

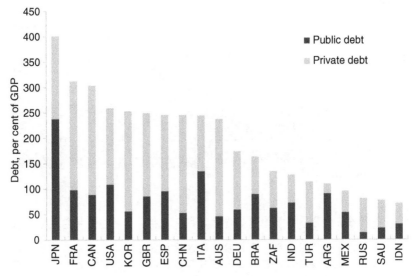

Figure 10 G20 global debt, 2019, per cent of GDP
Source: IMF (2020c)

corporations of up to 35% of GDP (see Figure 7). This comes on top of the pre-existing stock, which amounted to 20% of GDP in several European economies. If there is a major shake-out in the corporate sector post-COVID, significant losses may fall on the financial sector and/or governments. Finally, pension funds and life insurance companies may incur losses when interest rates stay low for long because their returns will not match their obligations. And they may lose money when interest rates rise substantially so that clients redeem these assets (whose market value has fallen) and seek higher returns (Deutsche Bundesbank, 2019). We will come back to these issues in Section 3.

2.5 Debt Sustainability: A Local and a Global Challenge

The preceding facts and analysis suggest significant sustainability risks for governments. A continuation of past debt dynamics with debt ratcheting up in each recession plus contingent liabilities from population ageing and risks in the financial system are in many countries quite concerning. The US public debt explosion that is predicted by the CBO is a case in point for the risks from debt servicing costs and social expenditure (see Figure 6). Many other countries show debt projections with similar dynamics.

In fact, sustainability risks are not limited to emerging and small advanced countries as in the past; they are of a global scale (Table 5). When taking a debt ratio of near or above 240% of GDP for total debt plus high public debt as crude benchmarks, the highly indebted G7 countries plus Spain comprise over 40% of global 2019 output. When you add the countries with high private debt (and near or above 240% of GDP in total debt), over 60% of the global economy should be considered as vulnerable. The share would rise further if we were to add the large emerging economies with very high public debt. In the euro area, the vulnerable countries comprise over 50% of euro area GDP, and the three large ones over 45%. This illustrates that very high indebtedness is a global and systemic, not just a local or regional, challenge.

2.5.1 Debt Sustainability Analysis in the EU

The 'rule-of-thumb assessment' of over-indebtedness presented above is confirmed by formalised sustainability assessments. The most prominent ones are those conducted by the European Commission (for the European Union) and the IMF but there are many countries that have developed advanced methodologies. In fact, the analytical tools and frameworks evolved hugely over the past decade after former 'early-warning' instruments had failed to predict the global financial crisis emanating from the United States and its mutation into fiscal crises in Europe.

Table 5 Share of highly indebted countries in global and euro area economy, 2019

Countries with public debt well above 100% or public and private debt around or above 240% of GDP in 2019	Total debt (public and private) in % of country GDP	Share of national economy in global economy	Share of national economy in euro area economy, high public debt countries
1) All IMF high-debt countries/all high-debt euro area 1/advanced countries (IMF)		62.2%	51.5%
United States	259	24.5%	x
Japan	401	5.8%	x
United Kingdom	249	3.2%	x
France	313	3.1%	20.3%
Italy	245	2.3%	15.0%
Spain	246	1.6%	10.4%
Canada	304	2.0%	x
2) IMF, high private sector debt only			
China	245	16.3%	x
Korea	253	1.9%	x
Australia	238	1.6%	x
3) Memo: other euro area high public debt			
Portugal	278	x	1.8%
Belgium	307	x	4.0%
Greece	289	x	1.5%

Source: IMF (2020c); World Bank World Development Indicators

1/ Countries as in IMF (2020c, fig. 1.1.1) (groups 1+2) and high-debt countries in the euro area (groups 1+3)

The European Commission framework as reflected in its latest assessment (European Commission, 2021) looks at three different time horizons: the short term (within one year), the medium term (ten years) and the long term (fifty years). The assessment is based on the European Commission's forecast for the short term. It relies on the Economic Policy Committee's medium-to-long-term growth, labour supply, interest rate and other assumptions applied to all members. For the long term, it looks at the Committee's and the Commission's ageing cost projections.

The short-term (or S0) indicator identifies the risk of fiscal stress in the form of i) a credit event, ii) a request for significant official financing, iii) default (including via high inflation) and iv) a loss of market confidence. It looks at about twenty-five fiscal, macro and financial indicators, gives them a different weight based on their respective signalling power estimated from a sample of past crises and then defines risk thresholds. The most highly weighted variables are the cyclically adjusted budget balance (−2.5% of GDP threshold), short-term debt (ca 13% of GDP), net debt (ca 60% of GDP) and the gross financing need of government (ca 15% of GDP). Private sector credit flows, the yield curve, the current account and household net savings feature prominently amongst the non-fiscal indicators. This analysis would have only missed 22% of past crises while leading to 23% of false alarms.

The 2021 short-term risk assessment shows eleven EU countries at the risk of fiscal stress in the following year (compared to zero in 2019 and seventeen in 2009) (Table 6). Again, the weight of euro area countries at high short-term risk is well above 50% of the euro area economy and includes the six countries with very high debt.

For the assessment of vulnerability over the ten-year horizon, the Commission looks at the budgetary adjustment that would be needed to make debt sustainable relative to a 'no-action' baseline scenario. 'Sustainable' is defined as bringing the debt to 60% of GDP within fifteen years. This medium-term (or S1) indicator is complemented by a debt sustainability analysis (DSA) that projects the debt ratio over the next ten years on the basis of the above-mentioned common projections and the assumption that primary balances will gradually reverse to pre-COVID levels.

In these projections, two facts are noteworthy. First, extremely low interest rates (based on market expectations!) lead to high contributions from inflation to bring the debt ratio down. The average debt-reducing effect is about 1½% of GDP per year for the coming decade (and a total of about 15% of GDP). Second, and despite this large favourable effect, public debt in the most highly indebted countries would not come down compared with 2020: in 2031, Belgium and France would feature public debt around 120% of GDP, Spain would experience

Table 6 Countries at sustainability risk, European Commission analysis

Risk matrix for EU countries	Short term (1 year) (S0)	Medium term (2031 horizon) (S1 and DSA)	Long term (2070 horizon) (S2)
High risk	Belgium Spain France Hungary Italy Cyprus Latvia Portugal Romania Slovakia Finland	Belgium Spain France Italy Portugal Romania Slovenia Slovakia	Belgium Luxembourg Romania Slovenia Slovakia
Medium risk		6 countries (including the Netherlands)	16 countries (including all large countries)
Low risk	15 countries	12 countries (including Germany)	5 countries

Source: European Commission (2021)

a further major increase to 140% and Italy would report 155% of GDP. Only Portugal's debt ratio would fall from 127% to 107% of GDP.

The sustainability analysis of the Commission based on the S1 indicator and the DSA finds eight countries at high risk. Apart from the five euro area countries that were already found at high short-term risks, this includes three Eastern European countries. Two of these are also in the euro area. Again, the share of these countries in euro area GDP is well above 50%.

For the EU and the euro area as a whole the Commission does not find high risks, despite very high average financing needs (about 20% of GDP in 2021–2) and high medium-term risks in countries including more than half the euro area's GDP weight. Public debt will rise slightly further from the 2020 average of 102% of GDP in the euro area until 2024/25 before declining to 98% by 2031. However, these figures do not include the €750 billion additional debt from the pandemic-related European debt programme 'Next Generation EU' (NGEU). European Union members agreed on this programme in the spring of 2020 to help the European post-pandemic recovery and the EU will issue additional public debt up to this amount in the coming years. This debt is also not included in national debt, even though the citizens of member countries will have to pay for it.

Finally, the Commission looks at long-term risks by assessing notably the fiscal costs of population ageing and the fiscal adjustment that would be needed to stabilise the debt ratio 'indefinitely' (S2). Based on the findings of the ageing cost assessment of 2018 (European Commission, 2018), the Commission sees five EU countries at high risk. France, Italy and Spain escaped this categorisation despite the DSA results as the long-term projections of ageing costs do not show any or only moderate additional expenditure increases.

2.5.2 IMF Vulnerability and Debt Sustainability Analysis

The failure to anticipate the global financial crisis and its main drivers also induced the IMF to significantly improve its toolkit for vulnerability and sustainability analysis. The assessment was widened from looking mainly at government debt to including banks, non-bank financial institutions, house-holds and the corporate sector. The financial vulnerability assessment is regu-larly portrayed in the IMF's *GFSR* while the *Fiscal Monitor* focuses on fiscal vulnerabilities.

The IMF's comprehensive analysis confirms the above findings and concerns about debt-related vulnerabilities. Of twenty-nine countries analysed, the IMF only shows two countries with low or medium-low vulnerability in the govern-ment, bank and corporate sectors. Six countries display medium-high to high vulnerabilities in all three sectors and some twelve countries feature vulnerable governments. The IMF does not reveal the names but the high-debt countries flagged by the IMF elsewhere (and here in Figure 10) provide a good idea and include most of the 'big' names in the advanced and emerging world.

In the April and October 2021 *GFSR*, the IMF reports a more granular picture of sector and regional vulnerabilities and their change relative to the global financial crisis. The high and hugely increased sovereign vulnerability com-pared with ten years ago stands out. Some 80% of governments were assessed as vulnerable compared with about 20% only ten years earlier. This means that, post COVID, there are few countries left that have significant fiscal leeway and, amongst them, few large ones.

The IMF sees a significant increase in vulnerabilities for non-financial firms and asset managers (see Figure 11). In many of its publications, the Bank of International Settlements (BIS) has warned repeatedly that this is the new Achilles heel of the financial system (BIS, 2018 and following Annual Reports). The March 2020 turmoil, with massive asset redemptions and liquid-ity shortages, is witness to the risks arising from run-prone shadow banking and

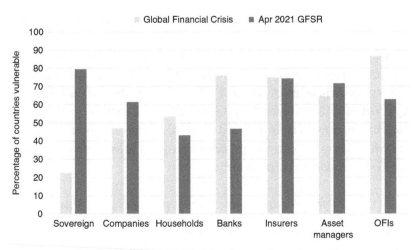

Figure 11 Global financial vulnerabilities, by sector

perhaps also international reserve managers (see Section 3.5). By contrast, the vulnerability of banks and other financial institutions declined, following significant efforts after the global financial crisis. Finally, the Fund does not see generally higher vulnerability in emerging economies than in advanced countries, except for banks – vulnerabilities are present more or less everywhere.

The IMF is in the process of introducing a new, more sophisticated debt sustainability analysis (IMF, 2021e). This will look at the near-term (one to two years), the medium-term (up to five years) and the long-term (up to ten years) horizons to get a better grip on liquidity and solvency risks. The medium-term analysis is based on three components: the first element is a debt fan-chart that assesses a country's debt-carrying capacity dependent on the quality of institutions. The second component evaluates the potential for financing stress via financing demand and financing space of the relevant financing sources (domestic and foreign, financial and non-financial sector). The third element is a set of stress tests related to banking crises, natural disasters, commodity prices and real effective exchange rate shocks, reflecting the global clientele of the IMF. Risk to central banks from potential losses from rising interest rates on government debt holdings are not considered, except when there is significant negative equity. The long-term analysis includes the foreseeable challenges related to population ageing, natural resources and debt amortisation needs.

The medium-term analysis is going to be most relevant for IMF advice and programme work. It will result in a probabilistic model that will yield three categories of countries: debt is sustainable with a high probability, debt is sustainable but not with a high probability, and debt is not sustainable. This analysis should also guide debt restructuring. The IMF also considers long-term risks by looking at the above-mentioned modules in a non-mechanical manner.

2.5.3 Merits and Limits of Debt Sustainability Analysis for the Post-COVID World

Why should we devote so much attention to the debt sustainability analysis of key international organisations? These approaches show the great progress that has been made in looking at public debt from a comprehensive and international perspective by applying modern approaches and tools. They capture the experience with sustainability risks up to the European fiscal crisis in the early 2010s. They show much more clearly the interdependence of public finances with risks elsewhere in the economy. They also take into account future risks that could already affect sustainability prospects and confidence today.

There are two important shortcomings. The first is quasi-technical and, at least to some extent, cannot be avoided. Probabilistic analysis (formally in the IMF and less formally in much of the European Commission assessment) by definition relies on our experience from the past. The variables included and their weighting depend on their predictive power for past crises. We are hence in a good position to win the 'wars' of the past.

However, there may be new variables to look at that should already be on our radar even if they cannot be used for statistical analysis. These new variables include the role of international capital flows due to asset management and sovereign reserve management, the distorted market signals due to central bank intervention (the European Commission hints at it) and the possibility of central bank losses, the 'ample' money supply (and money overhang), the likelihood of asset price bubbles in many countries, the effect of structural developments on future growth prospects beyond the 'knowns' such as ageing-related falls in labour supply, the unpredictable effect of high and higher spending on growth and finance, the unclear impact of decarbonisation on growth, spending and debt, and the fiscal and growth impact of more defense spending and protectionism in a strained geopolitical environment. We will discuss these points in the next section.

Second, and perhaps most importantly, debt sustainability only looks at country risks, treating all countries as 'small'. It does not take a global or systemic view. However, such an approach is not enough, given record debt, especially in the largest countries, and past events have shown this (Acharya et al., 2017). We already learnt in the 2010s that even small countries like Greece and Cyprus can be seen as having systemic relevance. The IMF and European countries argued as much when they activated the 'ultima ratio' for financial support: financial stability in the euro area as a whole was seen to be at risk due to problems in these small countries spreading to the larger ones.

This raises many questions on how prepared we are to anticipate the crises of the future. Which important determinants of fiscal risks have been missing in our analysis? How likely is it that the negative result of a DSA analysis 'automatically' leads to orderly debt restructuring? How relevant are our interest and flow-related stress tests when investors can shift hundreds of billions of dollars or euros within days? Do we sufficiently take into account spillover and spillback effects from contagion?

2.6 Conclusion

Public debt has reached record levels globally and especially in the largest countries. In advanced countries, it is on par with post–World War II highs and there is no prospect of a decline. Moreover, there are significant fiscal risks for the future, especially from population ageing, callable guarantees and potential financial crises in much of the advanced and emerging world. The need for 'decarbonizing' our economies and geopolitical conflicts compound these challenges. The pandemic has potentially 'eaten up' most of the fiscal buffers for future challenges and crises. Consequently, international observers like the IMF and the European Commission rightly point to significant vulnerabilities and sustainability risks in many advanced and emerging countries.

Debt has also potentially taken on globally systemic dimensions. Advanced countries with very high public and total debt comprise over 40% of global GDP and over 60% when countries with very high private debt are added. Highly indebted countries also comprise over 50% of euro area GDP. Probabilistic DSA models for individual countries do not capture systemic risks. Already in the global financial crisis, it had not been anticipated that trouble in global, systemic banks is different from that in individual, non-systemic banks which run into problems.

International organisations and many other observers identify the growing debt challenge. The IMF *World Economic Outlook* (IMF, 2021f) and the IMF *Fiscal Monitor* refer to 'historically high debt' that requires 'resolving debt overhangs' and 'reducing fiscal risks'. The OECD (2021b) calls for a 'thorough review of public finances', including 'all government expenditure', 'ensuring debt sustainability' and 'establishing budget processes that strengthen incentives ... [and] risk frameworks'. The IMF emphasises the importance of credible fiscal rules and frameworks for long-term debt reduction (IMF, 2021b).

However, there is little sense of urgency and no reference to the large country and global dimension. International organisations argue that continued short-term support needs to be 'calibrated to the cycle' and 'eventually' scaled back. Leading economists such as Blanchard and Krugman argue in the same vein (see Section 1.1). There is more explicit emphasis on private debt in emerging markets than on public debt (and further risks) in large (and especially advanced) countries. The IMF *GFSR* of April (and October) 2021 stresses the 'pressing need to act to avoid a legacy of vulnerabilities' in the corporate and financial sector of 'emerging countries (that) face daunting challenges'. Perhaps it is the fear of 'crying wolf' and its consequences that make many observers reluctant to talk about large country fiscal risks and the global dimension. Perhaps such risks are not considered relevant, given that interest rates have been very low for so long, and they are, thus, not on the radar. This discussion has argued that they should be.

3 Debt Sustainability: Further Risk Factors

> The real danger comes from encouraging or inadvertently tolerating rising inflation and its close cousin of extreme speculation and risk-taking, in effect standing by while bubbles and excesses threaten financial markets.
>
> (Paul Volcker, 2018)

3.1 Introduction

The post-COVID debt situation is hugely challenging globally but the numbers are especially disconcerting for the largest countries. Public debt is at record levels, similar to post–World War II highs, and high private debt, contingent liabilities such as guarantees, population ageing and risks from potential financial crisis add to this. Despite low interest rates and favourable financing conditions, limits do still exist and will be felt again at some point. Sustainability assessments are clear on this and point to high risks, especially in high-debt countries.

The global and large country dimension of public debt, however, is not on the radar of the 'mainstream' discussion. Existing methods of risk analysis are single-country-focused and backward-looking; they assume that very low interest rates will prevail for a very long time and they assume a quasi-automatic adjustment of the COVID-related spending and financing imbalances. Hence, analysts and policy makers do not see the potential for and implications of sustainability risks in the systemically important countries.

However, the problems discussed above are not the full story yet. We risk overlooking or at least under-estimating the impact from further challenges in the fiscal, growth, financial-monetary and international sphere.

First, higher public spending post COVID may simply not be financeable in several countries. Moreover, there are often deeper governance problems that hinder effective public spending, even if there was more money (Section 3.2).

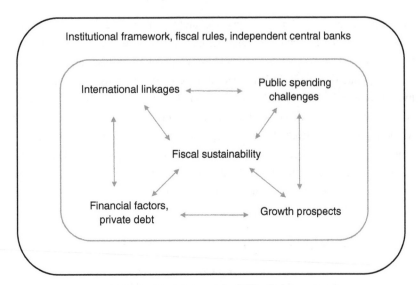

Figure 12 Debt sustainability linkages

Second, deteriorating framework conditions, climate change, protectionism and economic 'zombification' may lower economic growth prospects and increase cross-country divergence more than we currently expect (Section 3.3). Third, favourable financing conditions following ultra-low central bank interest rates and asset purchases have stimulated demand – but they have also compressed risk premia, encouraged risk-taking and inflated asset prices amidst strong money growth. Sustainability risks from financial instability, inflation and rising real rates and financing costs might be greater than we think (Section 3.4). Fourth, increased international financial interdependence has made markets, governments and central banks more vulnerable to shifts in confidence and international spillovers and spillbacks (Section 3.5).

All these factors are relevant for sustainable public debt and finances. Moreover, they are interdependent. Their smooth and benign interaction depends on credible institutional frameworks – sound fiscal frameworks, independent central banks and open markets – at home and abroad (see Figure 12). This holds all the more given the global scope of high debt, with the largest economies being amongst the most vulnerable.

3.2 Public Spending Size and Quality

3.2.1 The Importance of the Size of Government

More spending is very much en vogue post COVID because we all want more social, more investment-oriented and more resilient public policies. However, there are two important omissions in the argumentation for more spending. First, many countries' spending is much higher than needed – leaving room for savings rather than more spending – and it is higher than what is financeable. Therefore, more spending would often mean less resilience from a macroeconomic perspective.

Public expenditure was on average around 40% of GDP in advanced countries before the COVID-19 pandemic (whether above or below depends on the country sample). This was more than sufficient to provide a good institutional framework and high-quality public goods and services to citizens according to a large economic literature (see e.g. Afonso and Schuknecht, 2019; Schuknecht, 2020b). In fact, in many advanced countries, public spending ratios could have been much lower than they were pre-COVID, if only spending was more efficient and better targeted.

With COVID-19, government spending increased on average by a further 8 percentage points of GDP in 2020 to around 50% of GDP in advanced countries. The variance in public spending across countries, however, is huge (Figure 13). Ireland and Switzerland provided an excellent quality of life for their citizens with spending of around or a little over 30% of GDP. Singapore made do with even less. Italy and France spent about twice as much in 2020, around 60% of GDP, and the quality of public services was arguably not really better.

Other large countries also featured very high public spending ratios in 2020. The US and Japan came close to 50%, Germany, the UK and Spain posted spending of more than half of GDP. Some of this spending increase will reverse with the economic recovery, as Figure 13 shows, but it is not

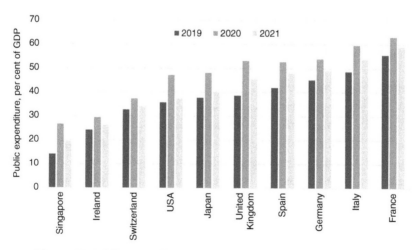

Figure 13 Public expenditure, general government, per cent of GDP
Source: IMF (2021a)

clear how much. The post-pandemic forecasts of the European Commission (2021) and the IMF *WEO* projections (IMF, 2021f) assume that primary balances and spending ratios revert to pre-crisis levels around the middle of the decade. However, this should not be taken for granted. Depending on growth and spending dynamics, a continuation on a higher spending path is not unlikely even before additional spending is considered. This is all the more plausible, given past experience with strong expenditure growth in good times and the widespread reluctance to re-apply fiscal rules after their suspension during the pandemic in many countries (European Fiscal Board, 2020).

The key question to ask, then, is whether the additional or, in many cases, even the prevailing spending ratio is financeable. High spending requires high taxes, and this means high tax wedges on labour and high consumption taxes. At some point, higher taxes may be counterproductive for revenue. Higher taxes also have political costs for policy makers. Especially in advanced countries, higher taxes often do not seem feasible, even if tax increases could provide more revenue.

There are two reasons why we should be concerned. First, in many high-spending countries, tax rates are already near or even above the revenue-maximising threshold. Akgun, Bartolini and Cournède (2017) show this for personal and corporate income taxes and value added tax (VAT). They estimate that revenue-maximising VAT rates are somewhere in the low 20s for most advanced countries and, considering a safety margin, even below 20%. Several high-spending (and high-debt) countries already have rates beyond that maximum (Figure 14a). The authors report similar findings for income taxes, where a number of governments tax important groups of workers near or above the revenue-maximising level (Figure 14b). This includes several of the high-spending-cum-high-debt countries.

There is more indicative evidence in this regard. When looking at international revenue statistics, it is a fact that no country in the post–World War II history of advanced countries has been able to collect revenue much above 50% of GDP in a sustained manner. Many countries seem to face a cap at much less than that. This may also be because tax increases have been politically too unpopular to garner the necessary parliamentary majorities. As a result, many countries would be unable to raise revenue by much and, thus, come closer to the economic maximum even if they wanted to.

What is the implication of this? Many countries had difficulties financing their public spending before COVID-19 and accumulated high debt. There is little reason to believe that this will change after the pandemic. If spending ratios and

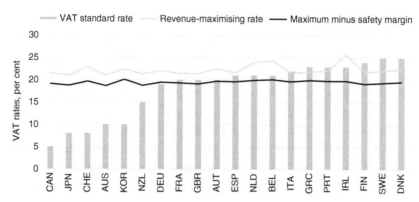

Figure 14a VAT standard rate vs revenue-maximising rate, per cent
Source: Akgun, Bartolini and Cournède (2017)

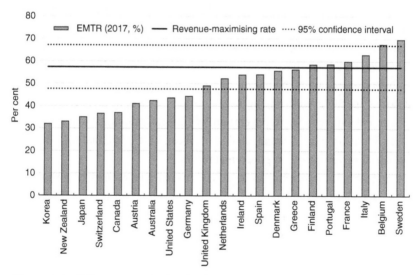

Figure 14b Effective marginal effective tax rates (EMTR) faced by workers
with wages equal to 167% of the country average and estimated revenue-
maximising rate
Sources: Akgun, Bartolini and Cournède (2017); OECD (2020a)

pressures are higher post COVID than before, this will also imply higher deficits
and more debt. Economists who argue for more spending tend to neglect this fact.

3.2.2 More Spending versus Better Spending

It is another fallacy that more spending necessarily means better government so
that, ideally, the additional spending finances itself via more growth. Proponents
of more spending typically assume that more spending solves health and social

problems, infrastructure and environmental challenges. However, today's problems do not exist because we did not know about them before COVID-19. They exist because in the past the incentives of policy makers in the context of imperfect institutions were not conducive to prioritising their solution.

More public money is not likely to change that unless we improve the governance underlying expenditure decisions. For example, a casual look at the data on spending dynamics in the past twenty years and at anecdotal evidence (e.g. for Germany) suggests that increases in spending on education have not been associated with an increase in education performance, as measured by PISA competence scores. Improvements in education governance were much more important.

Social spending is another example. In 2017, it absorbed almost one-quarter of GDP on average and over 50% of total spending in almost all advanced countries. Despite huge increases in health spending in all countries in the years and decades before COVID (there was simply no austerity whatsoever, despite claims to the contrary), systems were largely unprepared for the pandemic. Moreover, and worse, there are signs of the crowding out of productive spending by social spending (Schuknecht and Zemanek, 2020). There is, hence, a risk of social spending undermining fiscal sustainability both directly via higher deficits and indirectly via its adverse growth effects. Additional social spending in the future, as many demand, could then mean little additional resilience but less spending on other core government tasks.

On the whole, there tends to be no positive correlation between the size of public spending and government performance and often it is negative. This holds for the quality of public administrations, infrastructure, education and health, and for economic performance and stability (Afonso et al., 2005; Schuknecht, 2020b). Only income distribution indicators are moderately correlated with large social spending. But here again, the targeting and quality of the welfare state differs hugely: Korea, Switzerland and Ireland report a very similar income distribution (Gini coefficient) as Germany and France even though they report much lower social spending. The difference can be to the order of three: Korea spends about 10% of GDP, France about 30%.

Some people claim that decarbonisation to counter climate change requires more spending. This is true for adaptation measures such as storm barriers and dykes and managing the adverse impact of higher carbon prices on the poor. But the total effect on spending and the net effect on deficits and debt depend very much on the decarbonisation strategy. A market-based strategy relying on carbon pricing easily generates the revenue to finance remaining adaptation and mitigation measures while also minimising adverse social and growth effects. A strategy based on discretionary regulation and subsidies is likely to be less efficient and more prone to rent seeking. It will, thus, also be much more costly in terms of spending, growth and debt (see also Section 3.3).

The geopolitical tensions and the war in Ukraine that erupted just before this Element went to print highlighted the need for more defence spending in many advanced countries. The magnitude ranges between ½ and 1 per cent of GDP for countries with spending well below their commitment of 2 per cent of GDP. While substantial, this figure is small relative to the recent and planned spending increases in the social sphere. This underpins the need for better spending and for realizing expenditure savings.

Hence, the conclusion from the COVID-19 pandemic (and climate change as well as geopolitics) that we need more spending and debt is not convincing. There clearly is a need for better spending and more prioritisation. Low retirement ages raise debt ratios through higher spending and lower output. Some social programmes keep people in unemployment traps due to benefit withdrawal exceeding the additional working income, as many studies have shown. The complexity of social spending often undermines its effectiveness via poor alignment and even contradictory effects of different programmes. More civil servants can increase bureaucracy instead of promoting better services and opportunities. Big public investment projects too often constitute white elephants. Reinhart and Rogoff (2009) describe how the Latin American crisis in the 1980s emanated from over-indebtedness induced by the recycling of oil money mainly into infrastructure projects. Poor governance is at the root of the problem and this is not going to be solved by pouring in more money. We will come back to this point in the next section.

3.2.3 Competition from 'Small' Government Countries

Public spending also needs to be seen from the perspective of international competitiveness. Especially in Asia, there are several countries with low spending, low taxes and vibrant economies (Table 7). Public spending is on average and in many countries much lower than in advanced countries. Competition for international investment with these countries will increasingly be over human capital and not factories. Singapore and South Korea, for example, offer formidable business environments and a high quality of life with low personal taxes. It is perhaps no surprise that these countries' prosperity has been catching up rapidly and nowadays even exceeds that of many of their European peers.

The main difference to most advanced countries' spending patterns lies in the size of the welfare state. Productive spending on infrastructure or education, for example, is typically not much lower in these Asian countries, if at all.

Table 7 General government expenditure,
2019–20, % of GDP

	2019	2020
Advanced countries	38.6	47.4
Emerging countries	31.8	35.0
Asia		
China	34.1	37.0
India	27.1	31.0
Indonesia	16.4	18.2
Philippines	21.7	25.1
Singapore	14.1	26.6
Thailand	21.8	25.3
Russian Federation	33.9	38.8
Latin America		
Argentina	38.3	41.6
Brazil	37.3	42.7

Source: IMF (2021a)

Australia, Ireland and Switzerland also feature a greater emphasis on productive spending. Low spending and low debt will probably enable these countries to better master the challenges of the future, including population ageing and climate change.

Fiscal competition may in fact lower the growth and revenue potential of big government countries in the future through the human capital channel, if high taxes deter the smartest and most innovative people from living there (see also Section 3.3). Agreement on a minimum corporate tax rate will not change this to a large extent because competition is mainly over brains, not bricks, as mentioned above. Competition with lean states that also feature strong public services may, thus, have greater implications for the sustainability of high debt and big government in the future than most economists think.

3.2.4 The Timing of Adjustment

All in all, better, not more spending could square the circle between reducing spending, deficit and debt ratios and managing post-pandemic fiscal challenges. Better spending means that spending is better targeted to its objective (such as more effective education and poverty reduction) and more efficient in its execution. This requires strong fiscal institutions and governance (OECD, 2019a) and sometimes, private financing can come in (e.g. in infrastructure; see also Section 3.3). In many countries, less not more spending will be advisable. But when should the consolidation of spending start? The IMF, the OECD and many observers have been suggesting caution while uncertainty over the economic outlook persists.

At the same time, it should be avoided that another recovery passes without progressing towards sound public finances. In fact, the 2014–19 recovery was not used by high-debt governments to consolidate but to conduct very expansionary expenditure policies (European Fiscal Board, 2020).

Why is this important? First, Summers (2021), for example, argued that too much stimulus for too long causes an overheating of aggregate demand, which could (further) stoke inflation and rising debt service costs. The OECD (2021b) acknowledged the upside risk to demand emanating from a stronger consumption rebound also in Europe.

The second reason is structural: whilst budget constraints remain soft, government measures are increasingly likely to be captured by special interests instead of improving the quality of public finances. This was the experience of many countries in the past (Kornai, 1986) and undermines sustainability via lower growth.

Third, and perhaps most importantly, governments put their reputations at risk. If the perception grows that governments are not willing to return to principles of sound budgeting, investors are likely to become weary at some point. At that point, citizens might also lose faith in the ability of central banks to raise interest rates when needed if that risks turmoil in government finances – the classic case of fiscal dominance (see Section 4.5). It would be important to act earlier rather than later, well before that point is reached.

3.3 Growth Prospects in the Post-COVID World

3.3.1 Falling Growth Rates and Investment

Most economists do not seem to expect a change in economic growth prospects post COVID. Broadly unchanged long-term growth projections (e.g. by the European Commission and the IMF) underpin this expectation. However, there may be reasons to expect a further decline in potential economic growth for institutional and structural reasons that are not much on the radar of observers. If growth is over-estimated, public spending plans (which typically follow growth projections) will also be less sustainable. For the period before the global financial crisis, European countries had systematically over-estimated growth to the order of 0.5% per annum. This compounded to very significant expenditure and debt ratio increases (Hauptmeier et al., 2011).

The decline in economic growth and notably labour productivity growth has been a fact for decades in advanced countries. The OECD reported trend growth of around 3% and productivity growth of 1.5–2% for its members in the 1970s

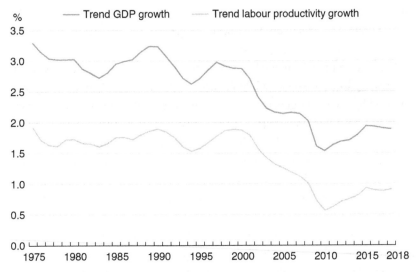

Figure 15 Trend real economic and labour productivity growth, OECD
Source: OECD

and 1980s before it declined to 1.5–2% and 0.5–1% respectively, in the 2010s (Figure 15). Much of this decline was not anticipated and, thus, led to overly expansionary expenditure policies.

Many economists suggest that lower growth and lower real interest rates are due to a so-called savings glut linked to demographics, high-saving Asia, a lack of investment opportunities and insufficient public (investment) demand. Looking at the facts, however, it may be less a generalised increase in savings than a decline in private investment that is to blame. The most significant change over recent decades, in fact, is the decline in private investment in advanced countries. Gross fixed capital formation fell by about 2 percentage points of GDP in the euro area, the US and Japan in the 2010s compared with the 2000s and almost all of this decline comes from private investment. The overall decline is somewhat less in Germany and the UK (Figure 16). In the euro area, lower public investment only makes up for 0.3% of GDP, or less than one-sixth, of this decline.

Moreover, it is not a shortage of public money that explains low and falling public investment, but lengthy bureaucratic and judicial procedures at the national and European level (KfW, 2020; Wissenschaftlicher Beirat beim BMWI, 2020). There is also much unused potential for involving the private sector in financing public infrastructure (Schwartz et al., 2020; Ruiz Rivadeneira and Schuknecht, 2019). This points to a deeper, institutions-driven malaise at the root of deficient public (and private) investment, as argued above. Tackling these institutional challenges rather than simply seeking more public money is likely to improve infrastructure, private investment and growth prospects.

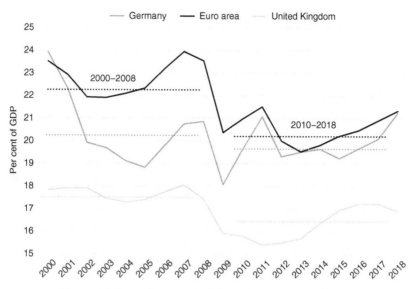

Figure 16 Gross fixed capital formation, per cent of GDP
Source: OECD

3.3.2 Framework Conditions for Confidence and Private Investment

Economic growth on the supply side is determined by people's willingness to work, invest and innovate. This willingness requires sound framework conditions – 'rules of the game' – for competitive markets, as generations of economists since Adam Smith have stressed. Innovation goes hand in hand with 'creative destruction' – the disappearance of uncompetitive firms – in competitive markets. Governments can promote growth and confidence when they set the appropriate framework conditions. This is an underappreciated social dimension of the market economy where a level playing field provides equal opportunity, enhances wages and increases social mobility (Aghion and Mhammedi, 2021). In Germany, this is called the 'social market economy' (Feld et al., 2021).

Unfortunately, the quality of framework conditions in many advanced countries has been declining over the past twenty years and probably even longer. The growing obstacles to investment more broadly, and infrastructure in particular, are important examples of this. When looking at rule of law and government effectiveness indicators, top countries have kept their positions but especially those competing with emerging markets have started falling back. Korea is now ahead of Portugal and Spain, and India and Indonesia have almost caught up with Greece as regards government effectiveness (Figure 17). Other Asian economies are also advancing, and Singapore tops the league.

The understanding of the importance of framework conditions and rules of the game seems to be declining. The IMF *WEO* of April 2021 makes no

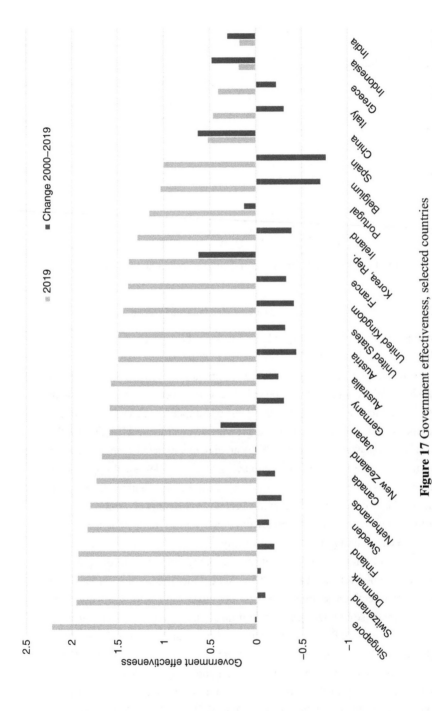

Figure 17 Government effectiveness, selected countries. The index measures the quality of public services, civil service, policy formulation, policy implementation and credibility

Source: World Bank World Development Indicators.

reference to it when discussing future growth but talks all the more about the role of government policies. There is a growing willingness to direct economic operations via subsidies or interventions in the belief that governments know how to pick 'winners'. However, history and landscapes are littered with such failed and costly attempts. If this trend prevails, it will not only reduce efficiency and growth directly but also stoke international conflict over 'unfair' competition and undermine the rules-based global economic order.

The choice of governance for international decarbonisation is going to be a litmus test in this regard. Decarbonisation is going to cost money in the short to medium term by definition, while in the long term, the positive effects will far outweigh these costs (OECD, 2021a). Companies and households will have to invest in less polluting production, traffic, heating, agriculture, etc. The key question is how this transition is going to be brought about: by a market-driven and efficient pricing process or by distortionary interventions, regulations, subsidies and punitive tariffs. This will determine whether there is a significant 'unanticipated' adverse growth impact from decarbonisation in the coming decades or not.

The need for action is enormous. The OECD reports so-called carbon pricing gaps by compiling data on the price of carbon emissions and the price equivalence of other measures (OECD, 2021a). It finds that all countries are far from a carbon price of 30, 60 or even 120 euros per ton. Some argue that 120 euros per ton is roughly the price needed by 2030 to achieve future targets. Large polluting countries, in particular, have hardly started to get there.

3.3.3 Zombification

The earlier discussion on 'creative destruction' and its positive distribution and growth effects is closely linked to concerns about growing corporate 'zombification'. During the pandemic, many firms have been rightly kept alive with the help of government guarantees, subsidies and moratoria on insolvency procedures. This helped to preserve jobs and companies and allowed a rapid restart as the pandemic began to fade. However, we do not know how many of these companies will be 'new zombies' that come on top of the many over-indebted, non-viable 'zombie firms' that already existed before the pandemic.

The share of zombie firms (firms with poor growth prospects not earning their debt service costs for two years) has been increasing broadly in tandem with declining interest rates and economic downturns in advanced countries (Figure 18). Moreover, the survival probability has increased from 60–70% in the early 2000s to over 80% in the later 2010s as banks (and regulators) engaged in widespread forbearance (Banerjee and Hofmann, 2020). This means that

Figure 18 Share and survival probability of zombie firms, selected advanced countries

Source: Banerjee and Hofmann (2020). Based on fourteen advanced countries

zombies do not just exist temporarily; there is a growing risk that they truly never die. It is very likely that the share of zombies is much higher post COVID. The fall in corporate insolvencies in most advanced countries during the pandemic at a time when many businesses had little to do is a clear sign of that. But the extent of the problem will be unclear until the dust has settled.

Current medium-to-long-term macro and growth projections do not consider the zombie challenge. Growth prospects will suffer if the challenge is not dealt with (ECB, 2021). By contrast, there may be upside potential from determined action. Adalet McGowan et al. (2017) found that solving the zombie problem of the mid-2010s would have led to investment gains of up to 1% and productivity gains of up to 1.4% in a number of advanced countries. The increased stock of potential zombies post COVID is likely to imply even greater gains.

3.3.4 Protectionism

Another important supply-side factor that could give rise to adverse growth surprises is trade policy. The amount of casual talk about re-nationalising supply chains and increasing autarky is astounding, all the more as the published motives are mostly unconvincing. Protectionism tends to reduce a country's growth prospects and resilience against future shocks.

Simulation results show that the price of protection can be very high. The OECD (2020b) found that protectionist policies that include 25% tariffs, 1% subsidies for renationalising industries and some obstacles to relocation would result in a GDP loss between 5% and 10% and export demand would fall by 5–30% (Figure 19). Note that the assumptions in these simulations look strong by today's standards but they are not strong when looking back in history. Tariff increases during the Great Depression were significantly larger, with devastating effects on trade, finance and the international economy.

Protectionism would also increase prices. The trade restrictions in the early phase of the pandemic gave a foretaste of this risk: the price of affected medical products increased by 7–40%. (Espitia et al., 2021). This is not relevant from a macroeconomic perspective when it is limited to a few medical product lines. But more broad-based protection would have stagflationary effects. In fact, growth prospects declined and inflationary pressures increased as the COVID-19 pandemic continued and especially as supply disruptions and uncertainty mounted with the start of the war in Ukraine.

3.3.5 Labour Supply and Growth Divergence

A further and well-predicted reason for a decline in trend growth is population ageing. Hence, in principle, this is not likely to cause surprises in countries' growth projections going forward. In fact, the European Commission anticipates this in its long-term projections. Euro area trend growth will decline to around 1% of GDP per annum in the period leading up to 2030. Labour supply in European countries will shrink on average by 0.3%, though there are significant differences across countries.

The challenge here is potentially more growth divergence due to labour migration which, in turn, would affect prospects for fiscal sustainability. Depending on their relative attractiveness, some countries will lose workers through emigration while others can improve their demographics with immigration. It is likely that countries that already do well economically and fiscally will attract labour from countries that feature weak public finances and poor growth prospects. Growing divergence from migration could affect both advanced and emerging economies, given that labour forces are expected to shrink almost everywhere in the advanced countries and in a number of emerging economies as well.

3.4 Financial-Monetary Factors

3.4.1 Financing Conditions, Risk-Taking and Bubbles

The prospects for fiscal sustainability are also linked to the financial and monetary environment. Ultra-loose monetary policies supported aggregate demand, jobs and inflation after the global financial crisis (Hartmann and Smets, 2018). However, there have also been growing side effects: Corporate and financial risk-taking increased (IMF, 2021d). Dynamic credit growth and

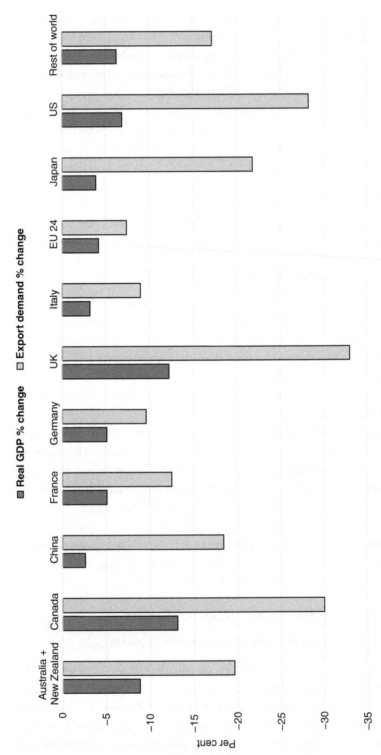

Figure 19 OECD METRO model simulations of GDP and export demand in a localised economy

Source: OECD (2020b)

asset price increases could sow the seeds of financial instability in the future (Detken and Smets, 2004; Agnello and Schuknecht, 2011). Government financing conditions were heavily affected by central bank asset purchases and an inflation debate started on the back of rising prices, cost pressures and inflation expectations.

Are we at a turning point, now that the forty-year financial 'bonanza' is behind us? After the great inflation of the 1970s, nobody would have predicted the decades-long bond market rally since then. Nobody would have predicted Japan being able to finance debt of 256% of GDP, spreads for high-risk bonds near historic minima, stock markets at ever new peaks and inflation hovering below official targets for years.

In fact, the financing environment was formidable for such a long time that it became hard to imagine much higher rates. In advanced countries, nobody below 45 or 50 has living memories of significant inflation. Long-term government bond rates in the USA have been falling from above 10% in 1979/80 to well below 2% in 2020/21. European government bond rates often started higher and declined further. German ten-year benchmark rates were in negative territory and Italian ten-year rates were mostly below those for US treasuries in 2019–21 (Figure 20). Moreover, spreads between government bonds in the euro area had fallen almost to historic minima in 2020/21 after rising dramatically during the European fiscal crisis.

Interest rates and risk premia in emerging economies also came down strongly, broadly in line with advanced countries. This reflects the growing willingness of investors to take risks in all markets and it shows the growing financial interdependence in 'one' global capital market (IIF, 2021c; OMFIF, 2021). All that happened despite much-increased public debt and debt issuance. No wonder that nobody worried.

The low-rate environment with increased risk appetite also allowed the seamless financing of more, and more low-quality, private debt. Private debt ratios, especially in the corporate sector, became very high in many advanced and emerging countries, including some of the largest ones (see Figure 2.10). In many countries, they grew well above the 160% rule-of-thumb threshold of the European Commission (see Section 2.5). The IMF *GFSR* (April 2021) reported declining average credit quality and increasing market risk. More than half of all corporate bond issues in 2018 were at the marginal investment grade of BBB (Çelik et al., 2019). The weighted average time for the next interest rate reset in debt fell from about six years in 2019 to little more than three years in early 2021 (IMF, 2021c).

These developments make governments and companies vulnerable when interest rates and risk premia rise. Moreover, high bond prices (due to low rates) coupled with record equity valuations raise the question of misalignments

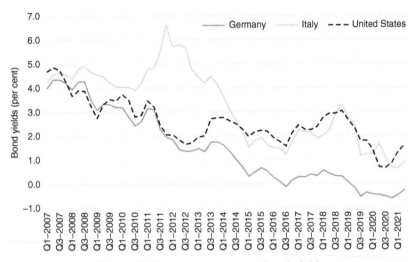

Figure 20 Ten-year government bond yields

Source: OECD

in asset markets. This could result in damaging boom-bust scenarios and financial instability mutating into fiscal instability. Booms embellish fiscal balances due to excess revenue and tempt governments into higher spending (Eschenbach and Schuknecht, 2004). Busts and financial crisis boost spending further and impact heavily on debt ratios. In Europe, this contributed to pushing several countries into fiscal crisis in the early 2010s (Schuknecht, 2020b).

There are signs of increasingly overpriced asset markets, despite some stock market corrections before this Element went to print. The IMF (2020a) found growing bond and equity market misalignments in advanced and emerging markets, after the market downturn of March 2020 had reversed quickly. The Official Monetary and Financial Institutions Forum (OMFIF, 2021) reports a sentiment of excessive risk-taking and overheating asset markets expressed by reserve and pension fund managers. Real residential house prices are showing significant 'froth', as central bankers call potential bubbles. Germany has been in a sustained, major upswing since about 2010, the United States since 2012/13 and the euro area as a whole since 2016 (Figure 21). By late 2020, real estate prices were approaching or exceeding the peaks before the global financial crisis.

Is this merely a bubble or even 'the mother of all bubbles'? Studies of earlier boom-bust cycles have developed metrics for bubbles (e.g. Detken and Smets, 2004; Jaeger and Schuknecht, 2007). Developments of recent years do not seem to suggest the highest alarms yet, but there are two reasons to be concerned. First, debt levels and zombification are at record levels and credit growth has been picking up. Although banks have reduced their vulnerability and increased capital, many suffer from low profitability, especially in Europe (Hartmann and

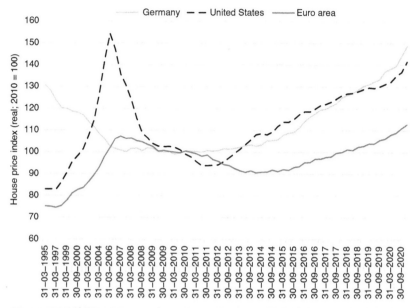

Figure 21 Residential property prices: Germany, United States and euro area
Source: BIS

Smets, 2018). Second, we started the rally from a higher level of private debt and asset prices and a lower level of rates and risk premia than previous booms. Hence, we do not know whether today's thresholds of 'frothiness' should be the same as in the past. Third, vulnerabilities and volatility risks have shifted to the non-bank financial sector, and we do not understand the potential interaction with banks and asset prices well. Surprisingly, these considerations hardly feature in the public debt discussion, despite past fiscal damages from boom-bust episodes.

3.4.2 Central Bank Challenges

Central banks and their monetary policies credibly anchored inflation expectations even in many remote corners of the world. This is a remarkable achievement and a huge success story. Still, we have mentioned rising inflation and the growing side effects via asset prices, investment quality and zombification. In addition, there are risks for central banks themselves. Financial risks arise from central banks holding very large amounts of government debt. In September 2020, up to 30% of central government debt was in the hands of central banks in the UK, the US and the euro area (Figure 22). In Japan, 50% of central government debt, almost 100% of GDP, was held by the Bank of Japan. These figures continued growing strongly thereafter.

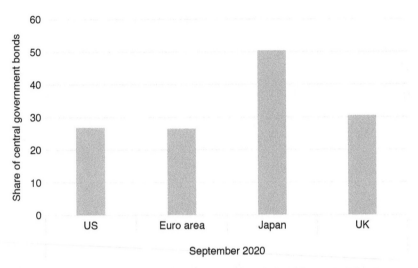

Figure 22 Share of central government bonds held by central banks
Source: BIS

The way in which financial risks can arise is complex (Deutsche Bundesbank, 2021). Central bank debt purchases, e.g. from banks, result in higher deposits by banks with central banks. Central banks pay interest on these deposits at the prevailing (central bank) rate. As long as interest rates on government bonds held by central banks are higher than the rate on central bank deposits, the latter make a profit. However, this can change when central bank rates rise and profits can decline quickly and significantly, as illustrated in Section 2.3. Over time, this can lead to negative equity and recapitalisation needs, which, in turn, hurt the financial independence of central banks and burden the government budget.

While these financial risks are real, the greatest challenge for central bankers should be the exit from ultra-loose monetary policies. When public debt is very high and private balance sheets weak, markets become nervous about tighter policies. Central bankers will experience opposition to raising interest rates or stopping government debt purchases even when inflation rises. If central banks raise rates, they may be blamed for government financing problems. If they do nothing, observers may ask whether this is a sign of fiscal dominance where central banks have to 'help' finance ministries to avert problems. Central banks may also come under pressure from the financial sector, which may fear defaults and valuation losses following higher interest rates. This is often referred to as the risk of financial dominance.

These arguments and concerns have been expressed in academic writing (e.g. Bordo and Levy, 2021; Diessner and Lisi, 2021; Heinemann, 2021) but they are not just academic. The Official Monetary and Financial Institutions Forum (OMFIF, 2021) reports that 65% of the surveyed central banks see preserving independence as one of their main challenges. According to the IMF (2020a), advanced country central banks bought the equivalent of 50–75% of government gross debt issuance between February and October of 2020. The largest central banks bought most net debt issuance well into 2021. The wealth-managing financial industry is often calling for a continuation of loose policies as they 'do their job' for their clients. But there are distributional implications from this and from central banks 'purchasing assets at high prices from a small group of relatively wealthy and informed investors' (Issing, 2021).

It is noteworthy that many emerging economies also conducted asset purchases as part of their monetary policies during the pandemic. The central banks of Poland, Hungary, Malaysia and Indonesia bought between 20 and 50% of government gross issuance between February and October 2020 according to the IMF. The programmes were quite successful in stabilising markets (Arslan, Drehmann and Hofmann, 2020) but they raise questions about exit and central bank independence in these countries as well.

3.4.3 Money and Inflation

Finally, we should discuss inflation prospects and the implications for fiscal sustainability. The inflation debate reignited quite suddenly in the first half of 2021 as headline inflation was rising faster than expected, and government support programmes were increased while the pandemic was waning. In the United States, inflation exceeded 5% in late summer 2021, while it exceeded 4% in Germany and the United Kingdom. Most observers still saw inflation as a transitory phenomenon at the time of writing, but the debate became quite controversial while the IMF acknowledged higher uncertainty (IMF, 2021g). With the supply disruptions related to the war in Ukraine, inflation and inflation prospects increased significantly further. It is therefore important to understand the arguments behind and implications of transitory versus more persistent inflation.

From a fiscal sustainability perspective, negative real interest rates with low inflation and even lower interest rates lead to a moderately lower real value of government debt (when abstracting from all other influences such as the deficit and economic growth). This is also often referred to as financial repression. High inflation and low rates reduce the real value of debt even faster because the 'old' debt stock contracted at low rates devalues more quickly. However, governments will need to issue new debt for financing their deficits and for refinancing old debt. This can quickly reverse the debt-reducing effect, depending on the average length of maturity of public debt and the interest rate response to rising inflation (including the above-mentioned effect from asset purchases).

Financing costs are more likely to adapt when inflation rises durably rather than temporarily. The reaction of market interest rates is likely to be stronger for countries where inflation expectations are less well-anchored and where public debt and other fiscal risks are high so that concerns about fiscal dominance and central bank action might arise.

Will inflation rise more durably or is it going to be transitory Until 2021, the latter view prevailed in many quarters: base effects from low energy prices in 2020, (hopefully) temporary effects from supply shortages and a demand over-shoot in certain sectors plus well-anchored expectations all suggested that inflation would 'normalise' quickly.

However, a number of factors could make the inflation increase that started in 2021 more durable and significantly affect financing costs for governments. First, population ageing, which reduces labour supply, together with a more rapid re-emergence of labour shortages, may re-ignite wage pressures more strongly and more durably. It may also reduce global savings as high-saving older workers turn into low-saving retirees (Goodhart and Pradhan, 2020). This (and the massive investment needs for decarbonisation and related industrial restructuring) could raise real (equilibrium) interest rates and change investor appetite towards risk. Borio et al. (2017) show a strong lagged correlation between dependency ratios and real interest rates for the past 150 years.

Second, governments are encouraging higher wages, especially for the low skilled, in many countries and surveys point to rising reservation wages in the USA (Federal Reserve Bank of New York, 2021) and infla-tion in tight labour markets is likely to lead to compensatory wage demands. Third, the adverse supply effects from zombification, supply shortages and protectionism may stoke cost pressures more durably than projected. Fourth, these demand and supply effects are likely to occur simultaneously in much of the advanced and emerging country world. This is a mirror effect of the inflation-dampening influence of global labour supply increases and market opening in the previous thirty years. Rather than producing disinflation, the global environment may, thus, contribute to global inflation pressure. Individual countries may find it difficult to decouple from this.

All this will not happen overnight but, together with the post-COVID inflation boost lasting longer and with concerns about debt sustainability and timely central bank action, it could unhinge inflation expectations. If that happens, the huge increase in money supply of the past twenty years

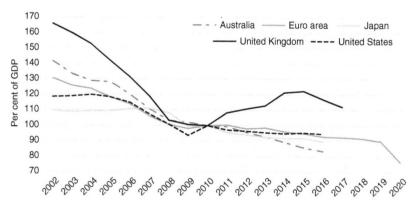

Figure 23 Broad money income velocity, M3, IMF definition,
selected countries
Source: IMF, *Monetary and Financial Statistics*

may unwind and the decline in monetary velocity may reverse as people 'flee' into consumption, into inflation-protected assets or even abroad. Money velocity, for example, almost halved in the euro area between 2002 and 2020 (Figure 23) and M3 (broad money) increased from 70% of GDP to about 130% of GDP over the same period. Other countries experienced similar trends. An unwinding money overhang would be a further boon to inflation that, in turn, would drive financing costs higher (Issing, 2021). If real rates rise and risk appetite wanes at the same time, the adverse financing cost effect would be stronger, especially for countries with high fiscal risks.

In summary, snapback risks from ultra-low interest rates and risk spreads, booming asset prices and financial stability concerns, central bank government debt holdings, rising inflation and rising real rates all potentially have implications for fiscal sustainability. The linkages from financial developments to public finances are even stronger with free international capital flows and financial interdependence.

3.5 International Financial Linkages

3.5.1 Economic and Financial Globalisation

Record public and private debt at the global level and especially in large countries has to be seen in the light of economic and financial globalisation. Trade and financial integration have fundamentally changed the interdependence between economies. This has brought about enormous gains in prosperity and opportunities. However, economic and financial spillovers and capital flow volatility have increased with it. Financial integration in particular is another Janus-headed phenomenon in our economies.

The post–World War II period features three important episodes of liberalisation. First, trade liberalisation started soon after World War II. Successive negotiation rounds until the 1990s established a rules-based world trade order that brought trade barriers down significantly. Second, starting in the 1970s, more and more countries liberalised their financial services and capital flow regimes (Abiad et al., 2010). International rules and regulations under the OECD, IMF and G20/Financial Stability Board auspices developed with a lag and only after major crises. Third, in the 1980s and early 1990s, China, other parts of Asia and Eastern Europe opened up. This gave trade and financial integration a several decades-long 'run' before the global financial crisis triggered some protectionism and was followed by a slow-down.

The evolution of policies and institutions is mirrored in the trade and capital flow dynamics. Trade integration started in the Western economies, followed by Japan, the Asian tigers and China. it is a marvellous account of how the participants rose out of misery and poverty. From little trade in the late 1940s, the ratio of exports plus imports over GDP had already reached 30% by 1970 (Figure 24). At that time China was closed. In the past fifty years, trade doubled or tripled again relative to GDP: in Germany from 30% to 90%, in the USA from 10% to 30% and in the world as a whole from below 30% to 60%. In most countries, the indicator stagnated after 2010. In China, trade openness had increased from zero to 65%, a huge value for such a large country, before the rapid growth of domestic demand resulted in a 'normalisation'.

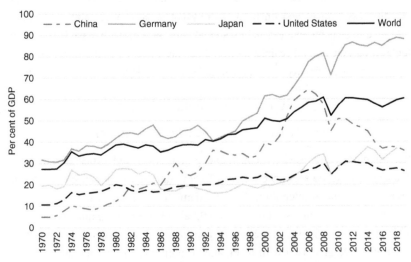

Figure 24 Trade openness (exports+imports/GDP)
Source: World Bank

3.5.2 Financial Globalisation

On the side of capital flows, it is very difficult to find comprehensive and representative data for longer periods. Following the widely accepted categorisation into direct investment (significant equity), portfolio investment (small equity and bonds) and other investment (bank lending), and looking across regions, one can derive a similar indicator for capital flows as for trade (Borio and Disyatat, 2011 and BIS). The sum of inflows and outflows for these three categories increased enormously before the global financial crisis from well below 10% of GDP in the early 1990s to over 30% in 2007 (Figure 25).

With the global financial crisis, capital flows 'crashed' to near zero in 2008 and 2009. They recovered gradually in the following years but remained significantly below the pre-crisis peak. This is consistent with the stalling trade-openness indicator and may reflect a degree of 'saturation' in trade and financial integration as well as some protectionist tendencies. Advanced countries were by far the most important group but emerging Asia posted major increases. In the 2010s, it accounted for roughly 20% of all capital flows.

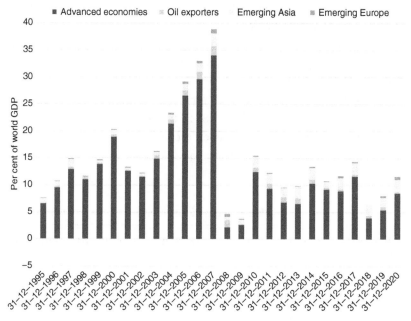

Figure 25 Gross capital flows, as a percentage of world GDP
Sources: Borio and Disyatat (2011); BIS
Note: Sum of inflows and outflows of foreign direct investment (FDI), portfolio and other investment in % of GDP.

These numbers show the annual gross flow figures, which are much more volatile than net flows and current accounts on which traditional macroeconomic analysis has focused (see also Eichengreen, 2016). They illustrate the significant potential for economic and financial spillovers across countries since the opening of capital accounts in the 1970s and 1980s. However, even these figures under-estimate the short-term volatility in capital flows. Annual gross flows may disguise much more intra-year and even daily change.

It is worth assessing in a bit more depth the potential for capital flow volatility. A good measure of integration is the stock of international credit as measured by the BIS. In September 2018, the total stock was US$ 30 trillion or 37.6% of global GDP (Table 8). This is a huge number. Given total global credit of about 250% of global GDP in that year, about one-sixth of it was international. Bank loans comprised 40% of the total or 16.3% of global GDP, with almost 10% of GDP cross-border lending and 6.4% foreign currency debt. The remainder of US$ 17.5 trillion was debt securities (bonds) held by banks and non-banks.

Of course, not all of this debt can turn into volatile capital flows overnight but a significant share can. This illustrates the importance of international finance as a source of crisis in high-debt countries when much credit is sourced internationally and in foreign currency.

The BIS proposed another way of looking at debt stocks and volatility risks. As mentioned, the global stock of private and public debt was 250% of global GDP or US$ 200 trillion in 2018 (Figure 26). About half of this, or US$ 100 trillion was financed through channels other than banks—asset managers etc. (second column). About half of this – US$ 50 trillion or ca 70% of world GDP – was invested in so-called run-prone assets according to the BIS (third column). This includes all those assets that can be liquidated relatively quickly. The chart

Table 8 International credit

	Trillion $	**% of global GDP**
Total	30.7	37.6
Bank loans	**13.3**	**16.3**
Cross-border	8.0	9.8
Local in foreign currency	5.3	6.4
International debt securities	**17.5**	**21.3**
Held by banks	4.7	5.7
Held by non-banks	12.8	15.6

Source: BIS, *Quarterly Review* (September 2018)

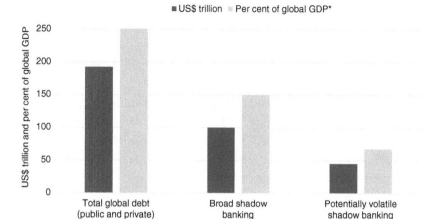

Figure 26 Total global debt and the role of shadow banking
Sources: IMF (2018) (debt); BIS (size of shadow banking)
Note: 'Broad shadow banking' refers to credit/assets managed by non-bank financial sector in Financial Stability Board member countries (85% of global GDP). 'Pot. volatile' implies potentially run-prone.

illustrates the huge magnitude of assets that could start to 'run' (domestically or internationally) when confidence is lost.

3.5.3 The Changing Nature of Financial Turmoil

With the European fiscal crisis of the early 2010s, advanced countries had to wake up to the fact that markets can treat them like emerging economies and that confidence loss could also affect them. Of course, people had only forgotten that this was not a new phenomenon: the UK had to go the G10 and the IMF in 1976 to cover its financing needs. The USA issued foreign currency bonds (Carter bonds) in the late 1970s when confidence in the dollar faltered. The post-Bretton Woods turmoil of the 1970s, however, involved rather small amounts of money, as capital markets were largely closed and the balance of payment was still the most important trouble indicator. The United Kingdom loan by the G10 amounted to US$ 5 billion, 2% of UK GDP, before this was replaced by an even smaller IMF arrangement.

This was very different in the late 2000s when a number of European countries experienced turmoil. Market participants realised that the common currency was for 'real' and euro area countries had maintained responsibility over national debt without the possibility of regaining competitiveness (and strengthening growth) via adjusting the exchange rate – as they had frequently done in the past. Large-scale banking crisis coupled with weak competitiveness and deteriorating fiscal prospects mutated into fiscal crises, as mentioned in Section 2.3. Confidence declined, capital flight set in and the intra-Eurosystem central bank credit line, called 'Target', swelled to several hundred billon euros. European countries and the IMF created rescue pack-ages also worth several hundred billion euros. IMF financing of 13.8–15% of GDP was complemented by European funding of 25% of GDP for Ireland and 30% for Portugal (Table 9). The Greek programme 'cost' 300 billion euros or over 150% of its GDP.

Ten years later, the main source of potential turmoil may have shifted again, from banks to non-bank financial actors. The 'dash for cash' financial turmoil in March 2020 may be indicative of that. It brought trouble to the doorsteps of the United States Treasuries market – the largest and most liquid debt market in the world. Markets reacted even faster and more strongly than ten years earlier. Rapid central bank action prevented spillovers to other parts of the financial sector and government finances. Events at the time almost read like an action movie.

In March 2020, when COVID-19 became a pandemic, investors panicked. In advanced countries, they withdrew US$ 200 billion from money market funds. Money market spreads (Libor-OIS) increased to 120 basis points, a sign of

Table 9 The size of international support programmes

		Amount approved (billion SDRs) 1/	Amount approved (% of GDP) 2/	Additional European financial support (% of GDP) 3/
Argentina	2018	40.7	11.2%	
Greece	2012	23.8	14.9%	135.9%
Portugal	2011	23.7	15.0%	30.1%
Ireland	2010	19.5	13.7%	25.6%
Argentina	2001	16.9	8.7%	
Korea	1997	15.5	3.8%	
Thailand	1997	2.9	2.6%	
Mexico	1995	12.1	4.9%	

Sources: IMF members' financial data; GDP from World Bank

1/ SDR=Special Drawing Right, a composite of the most important global currencies.

2/ GDP of respective country in indicated year.

3/ Some non-European countries, such as Mexico, also received limited additional financial support.

significant funding stress (Eren et al., 2020). Over-leveraged hedge funds liquidated huge amounts of assets, including US government bonds to a magnitude of US$ 80 billion, to stay afloat. At the same time, bond dealers could not accommodate the lack of demand so that market turnover declined while futures spreads increased strongly (Schrimpf, Shin and Sushko, 2020). Money flowed out of emerging economies and central banks started to liquidate some of their US Treasuries reserves. Sovereign bond spreads spiked and significant bond outflows occurred amidst depreciating exchange rates (Hofmann, Shim and Shin, 2020). All this happened within days.

Central banks reacted quickly to calm the situation. They conducted major asset purchases and installed international swap lines (open credit lines) and repo lines (liquidity against securities). Some of the drama is reflected in Figure 27. In the first quarter of 2020, there were massive redemptions of US Treasuries in the order of US$ 600 billion. This was more than absorbed by the

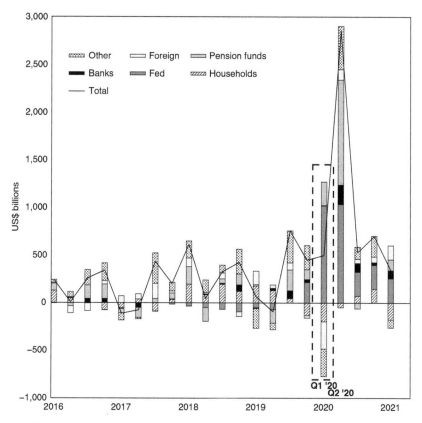

Figure 27 Issuance of US Treasuries vs demand by sector, in US$ bn
Source: IIF, quarterly data

Federal Reserve; pension funds were the only other net buyers of Treasuries (Vissing Jorgensen, 2020). 'Other' investors (including hedge funds) and foreigners (including central banks) were the main sellers. In Europe, it was also central banks that helped stabilise markets (Havlik et al., 2021).

From a forward-looking perspective, the events in March 2020 foreshadow a possible way in which future crises may unfold. Confidence loss will not manifest itself in a slow-moving process with a drawn-out tug of war between governments (which should act) and central banks (which do not want to overstretch their role), as was still the case in the European crisis. Markets may move extremely fast so that central banks will (have to) act to prevent mayhem as governments are too slow (and perhaps unwilling or unable) to do so.

There are potentially further lessons that are worth mentioning from a fiscal-financial perspective. The first two relate to emerging economies. Foreigners reduced their holdings of local currency bonds while especially domestic corporates increased domestic currency financing (Figure 28). Note the relative size of the markets: the local currency bond market of the represented countries is about four times the size of the borrowing in foreign currency. This is positive for market resilience and de-coupling prospects in the future because many crises in the past had their origin in very high foreign currency borrowing. Local currency financing and the mobilisation of domestic savings reduces the risk of contagion-related turmoil.

Second, stress-driven capital outflows seem to correlate strongly with country-specific fiscal situations. Norimasa et al. (2021) show that the outflow of capital from emerging economies in times of stress was much higher in countries with high debt. In fact, low debt was seen as correlating with inflows. Macro-prudential policies can help via well-regulated and stable domestic financial sectors and capital flow measures. However, sound public finances seem to be the best insurance for being on the 'safe' side of international financial contagion.

The third development concerns both safe-haven advanced countries and emerging economies and warrants further reflection. The high US dollar reserves of many emerging countries in Asia represent an important 'turmoil-insurance'. Asian countries (especially China) hold about US$ 5 trillion or 40% of global exchange reserves. This is the 'extraordinary privilege' of the US dollar at work and the United States benefits from the resulting dollar seignorage and safe-haven status. However, in March 2020, it proved to be a source of spillback as central banks divested several hundred billion dollars' worth of US Treasuries. As long as liquidity of and confidence in dollar instruments remain high, US dollar reserves remain an effective insurance instrument. This argument also holds to a lesser extent for the other reserve currencies.

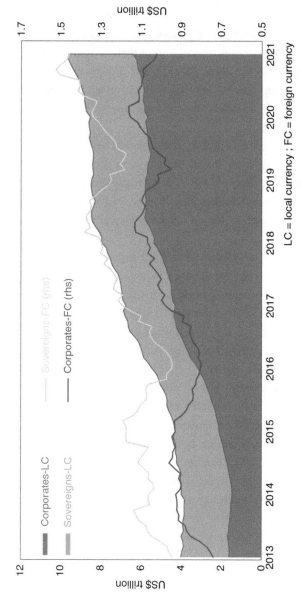

Figure 28 Local vs foreign currency debt by emerging market borrowers

LC = local currency ; FC = foreign currency

Source: IIF

3.5.4 International Safety Nets and Circuit Breakers

International capital flows are, hence, a blessing and they can become a 'curse'. The global community has developed three main instruments to mitigate openness-related risks and act as circuit breakers in or before crises. The first is international reserves, as discussed above, where the dollar dominates by far but a few other currencies also play a role (notably the euro, but also the pound, yen, Swiss franc and Renminbi). Reserve managers expect that the Renminbi will gradually play a growing role in the future (OMFIF, 2021). How the freeze of much Russia's foreign exchange reserves in early 2022 will affect the safety and liquidity perception of the US dollar and central bank reserve policies is an important, open question.

Second, macro-prudential measures are a well-established way to help manage capital in- and outflows. However, macro-prudential measures can only do so much. They may help with undue volatility and externally driven challenges such as excessive capital inflows. But they cannot 'solve' adverse confidence effects from sustainability concerns following major policy errors and unsustainable public finances.

International financial safety nets operate as a third 'insurance' instrument. They help countries correct and improve domestic policy regimes and, thereby, bridge confidence gaps in international financial markets until reform programmes take hold. The IMF is at the centre of this system, complemented by multilateral development banks, regional support schemes such as the European Stability Mechanism (ESM) and national or regional central bank-based support.

Economic and financial globalisation and rising public and private debt have hugely increased international financial support needs, as shown above. Overall safety nets also increased enormously. The IMF's effective lending potential stands at roughly 1 trillion dollars. The ESM can mobilise up to 500 billion euros. These are very large numbers that taxpayers are backing. But compared with total international credit and the potential for short-term market movements, and compared with the financing that would be needed if major economies got into trouble, they are not so large. Moreover, it is politically costly to activate these funds. It is no wonder, therefore, that the burden on central banks to deal with all forms of turmoil has increased. Their swap lines or asset purchases are much faster and potentially larger than inter-governmental support.

The credibility of inter-governmental and central bank safety nets hinges on the credibility of the anchors of the system, and notably the G7 countries. Most of these countries are very highly in debt. If one or several of these countries became a liability rather than an asset, international spillovers would be huge and safety nets could not cope. This should not be an irrelevant consideration.

3.6 Conclusion

The previous section argued that public debt and fiscal risks are very high globally. They are at risk of being unsustainable, including and especially in the largest economies. This section discussed further factors that increase fiscal sustainability risks but that do not always seem to be on the radar of analysts and policy makers. These concern public spending, growth prospects and the financial and international sphere.

First, high public spending ratios post COVID may not be financeable in several countries. They are also a symptom of deeper governance problems that hinder higher quality public spending. Second, growth prospects may be poorer than expected due to deteriorating framework conditions for investors, zombification of the corporate sector and protectionism. Third, low interest rates and risk spreads boosted demand but they also encouraged risk-taking, private debt and rising asset prices which, in turn, may have stoked fiscal sustainability risks via moral hazard, boom-bust cycles and rising financing costs for government. Population ageing and decarbonisation-related investment needs may raise real interest rates. Fourth, financial globalisation and interdependence have hugely increased the volatility of capital flows, which could interact in adverse and unpredictable ways with high debt and sustainability risks. The interaction of fiscal risks with these factors could also weaken the credibility of our institutional frameworks that underpin stability and confidence.

Debt and sustainability risks will eventually need to come down one way or another. There are four possible scenarios for this correction, displaying varying degrees of attractiveness: consolidation and reform, default, financial repression and destabilisation. These scenarios will be discussed in depth in the next section.

4 Scenarios of Debt Reduction

Why did no one see it coming?

(Queen Elizabeth, November 2008)

No country, however strong its fundamentals, can insulate itself from the effects of financial turmoil.

(Lee Kuan Yew, 1998)

4.1 Introduction

Section 2 presented the facts on global debt and risks post COVID and the significant concerns about the sustainability of public finances in many countries. Unlike in the past, however, the most highly indebted and potentially vulnerable countries are large and include the biggest global economies.

Section 3 argued that sustainability risks might be even graver than is commonly assumed. In quite a few countries, there are calls for more spending post COVID, although more spending may be not financeable and of low quality. Growth prospects are potentially weaker than projected. Financial distortions have increased instability risks, and inflation and financing costs may rise more persistently than expected. Moreover, international interdependence and contagion risks are greater than in the past. This goes hand in hand with growing concerns about the credibility of our institutions – fiscal, monetary, international – which are essential for confidence.

There are good reasons to argue that debt and fiscal risks will ultimately have to come down and there are, basically, four scenarios. The first scenario assumes debt reduction via fiscal consolidation and reform. There are some very successful precedents over the past decades. This path is more likely to be chosen by smaller countries. Second, countries can reduce their debt burden via default in what is called a 'debt workout' (IMF, 2021e). This has happened time and again in the past as well. Mechanisms are emerging that could make it more orderly and less damaging. However, it is not likely to happen in large countries.

Third, moderate inflation and low interest rates can reduce the real value of public debt. The past has known several such episodes of gradual debt reduction via financial repression. De facto, this is happening in the early 2020s in many advanced countries. Fourth, there is a risk scenario of financial repression becoming more destabilising as policy makers make mistakes and lose control. Economic history has known many episodes of debt crisis emerging in that way.

It seems worthwhile to understand better what these four scenarios would imply. Historical experiences often hold useful lessons about parallels and differences that may be relevant for the present. It is also worth discussing the political economy that affects the 'if' and 'when' of these scenarios to better understand how likely they are for which countries. Even if this approach does not remove the profound uncertainty over the future course of debt and debt reduction, it can help improve our understanding about possible ways forward. This may reduce the risk that, one day, Queen Elizabeth will yet again have to ask, 'Why did no one see it coming?'

4.2 Scenario 1: Consolidation and Reform

4.2.1 Describing the Scenario

The first scenario of debt reduction is based on the pursuit of fiscal consolidation and reform. It is worth recalling that fiscal stimuli during the COVID-19 pandemic (and the global financial crisis) were essential to support demand

and post-crisis growth prospects, but that implied a major increase in public debt. The challenge lies in using the recovery to break the unsustainable upward trend of recent decades and regain fiscal soundness.

With economic recovery in many countries, an undue delay is not advisable (see also Section 3.2). High-debt countries, in particular, would need to aim for broadly balanced budgets over the medium term so as to bring about a significant debt reduction momentum. This implies a significant (though by no means impossible) adjustment effort in the coming years. For 2022, France, Spain, Italy and the United States still expect large structural deficits of 4% of GDP and more, while the output gap will already have closed or be on its way to closure (European Commission, 2021). Large imbalances in some emerging economies – the IMF sees China's and India's deficit at 9–10% of GDP in 2022 – also suggest ambitious adjustment and reform.

4.2.2 A Simulation Exercise

Fiscal consolidation and reform make all the difference for the public debt path (Figure 29). The impact can be seen in a simple simulation exercise for a hypothetical 'average' G7 country with a starting debt of 140% of GDP. We assume that the fiscal balance improves by 1 percentage point per annum from a starting point of −4.5% in 2022 (t0) to −0.5% in 2026 (t4). Reforms raise the real economic growth potential moderately from 0.5% to 1% per annum while the real interest rate remains at −1% (broadly many countries' experience in the recent past and market expectations).

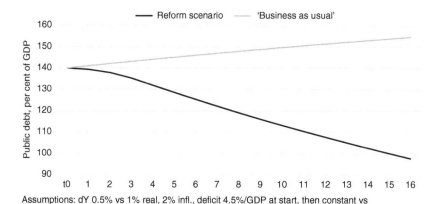

Assumptions: dY 0.5% vs 1% real, 2% infl., deficit 4.5%/GDP at start, then constant vs declining in 4 years to 0.5%, then constant. Starting debt 140% of GDP, real r = −1%.

Figure 29 Reforms vs 'business as usual' in a high-debt country, public debt per cent of GDP

Source: Own calculations

In this scenario, the debt ratio will decline as of 2024 (t2). It will have fallen by 27 percentage points of GDP within ten years and by 40 percentage points within fifteen years. It would still be at 100% of GDP then, but the solid downward path would be a strong, positive signal and a remarkable achievement. The simulations show that it will take a long time to bring down debt – policy makers will need much tenacity and a 'long breath'.

By contrast, if the starting point of a structural deficit of −4.5% of GDP was maintained for the next fifteen years and the economic growth record did not improve, the debt ratio would increase further even if interest rates stayed highly negative in real terms. In fifteen years' time, the debt ratio would be well above 150% of GDP.

Of course, these simulations are only an illustration, but they show the strong debt-reducing effect of consolidation and reform. Note also that the main effect here comes from deficit reduction; the growth increase by ½ percentage point per annum helps but it plays a modest role. Much stronger growth, of course, would bring debt down faster.

4.2.3 Experiences with Consolidation and Reform

All economists rightly agree on two things: fiscal consolidation needs to be growth-friendly and it needs to be embedded in a credible medium-term framework. But what is the most growth-friendly reform package? It is worth referring back to Section 3 for some historic experiences.

As regards the choice between tax and expenditure-based deficit reduction, there is a clear case for the second. Given very high expenditure ratios and correspondingly high taxes in many countries, there is often little room to raise revenue from higher taxes at all. And even if there is, the distortionary and growth-reducing effects from more taxes are likely to thwart the debt-reducing effect of such consolidation. Alesina et al. (2019) provide ample evidence for this claim. However, this does not speak against tax reform: in many countries, tax systems are inefficient and overly complex, and revenue-neutral improvements may contribute to debt reduction via higher growth.

This leaves the option of expenditure adjustment for tackling high debt. Government budgets of 40–60% of GDP, as featured in advanced countries post COVID, all have significant scope for expenditure reduction through efficiency gains. But it is worth differentiating to make sure that governments trim the fat and not the meat. Spending on government bureaucracies and on poorly targeted social spending has increased substantially in many countries over the past decades and provides much scope for savings. At the same time, the public debate rightly emphasises the need for productive public investment and skill formation that would also crowd in private capital spending. Productive spending on investment and education can and should, therefore, be prioritised, as some countries plan to do. Defence spending will need to rise in some countries as well. As mentioned, greater financial involvement of the private sector in infrastructure financing can fill an investment gap without higher public spending.

Second, governments should undertake fiscal consolidation as part of comprehensive reforms that strengthen the structural growth prospects of the economy (Hauptmeier et al., 2007). Moreover, a credible institutional framework for fiscal policies and budgeting enhances the effectiveness of spending and the prospects for fiscal sustainability (OECD, 2019a, 2019b on budget institutions; Heinemann et.al, 2018 and Gründler and Potrafke, 2020 on fiscal rules, notably in Europe).

This approach will also rebuild our economies after the pandemic. It means more jobs, more opportunities, an additional downward impetus on debt and a better chance to master future challenges such as decarbonisation, geopolitics and population ageing. It will lead to less bureaucracy, lobbying and crony capitalism. There will be better public services and more social cohesion and trust (Feld et al., 2021; Hank, 2012). In fact, this is the relation between government and the market that social market economists from Adam Smith onward have had in mind – not some form of unregulated, anti-social capitalist anarchy, as many critics claim.

4.2.4 Case Studies of Successful Adjustment

Many countries have demonstrated that comprehensive expenditure adjustment and reform is very successful with few, if any, harmful social effects. Many advanced countries undertook such reform in three waves in the 1980s, 1990s and 2010s. All reform waves started in crisis or near-crisis periods. At the starting point, fiscal deficit ratios were often over 10% of GDP and expenditure ratios averaged over 50%. Schuknecht (2020b) and Schuknecht and Tanzi (2005) describe the experiences for four countries in the 1980s, three countries in the 1990s and five in the 2010s. In the three waves, expenditure ratios declined by 8–13 percentage points of GDP and deficits by 6–10 percentage points in these country groups (Figure 30). This is more than the additional adjustment needed in many countries post COVID.

The seven countries that brought public spending down significantly in the 1980s and 1990s focused their efforts very strongly on the less productive spending categories, including transfers and subsidies (Table 10). Public investment spending 'only' declined in three of the seven cases and by much less than

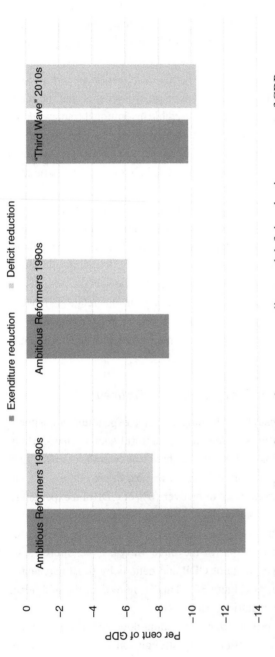

Figure 30 Expenditure reforms and average expenditure and deficit reduction, per cent of GDP

Source: Own calculations; Schuknecht and Tanzi (2005); Hauptmeier et al. (2007)

Note: For 1980s and 1990s, reduction between expenditure peak and 2002, for 'Third Wave' between expenditure peak and 2017.

Table 10 Total expenditure, year of maximum spending ratio and change until 2002, per cent of GDP

	Maximum public expenditure ratio	Year of maximum	Change maximum–2002	Thereof: Transfers & subsidies	Thereof: Investment
Belgium	61.0	(1983)	-10.5	-4.0	-2.3
Canada	52.8	(1992)	-11.4	-7.0	-0.5
Finland	60.4	(1993)	-10.3	-5.4	0.0
Ireland	49.8	(1982)	-16.4	-3.1	-0.7
Netherlands	58.7	(1983)	-11.2	-7.7	0.0
New Zealand	56.5	(1985)	-14.9	-8.0	0.1
Sweden	68.0	(1993)	-9.7	-5.2	-0.5

Source: Schuknecht and Tanzi (2005)

in other categories. Belgium, Ireland, New Zealand and the Netherlands, which had started their reforms in the 1980s, experienced an increase in real economic trend growth by 1.5 percentage point per annum over time. The public debt ratio came down by 30 percentage points over the following fifteen years.

Sweden, Finland and Canada started their reforms in the 1990s. They also brought down debt markedly in the following fifteen years amidst more robust growth. Income distribution became modestly more unequal, but strong income and employment gains benefitted the poor significantly (Afonso et al., 2005; Schuknecht, 2020b; on Sweden and Finland, see also Jonung, Schuknecht and Tujula, 2009).

The economic reform wave of the 2010s was more successful than its critics claim. Four of the reform countries, Ireland, Portugal, Spain and the United Kingdom, developed very favourably over the recovery of the 2010s. They showed much more economic dynamism than the non-reformers of France, Germany and Italy. Only Greece was an outlier (Figure 31). Moreover, income distribution as measured by the Gini coefficient became more equal in Ireland, Portugal and the United Kingdom whereas it deteriorated in the three non-reforming countries plus Spain and Greece (Figure 32 and Schuknecht, 2020b).

Memories tend to be short amongst economists and policy makers. Few remember the success stories of the 1980s and 1990s. Few remember that Germany was in deep trouble before their expenditure-based reforms in the early 2000s. Ireland, Portugal and Spain should receive much more praise for biting the bullet after the global financial crisis. But there are two common traits worth stressing. First, it is important to take the reforms up to balanced budgets and not stop with a significant remaining deficit. Otherwise, debt will decline little or even increase further during recoveries, as seen in many advanced countries in the past. Second, growth supports the 'mathematics' of debt reduction but it is no substitute for consolidation. All the earlier success stories and, more recently, Ireland, Germany and Portugal experienced significant debt reduction on the back of broadly balanced budgets and reasonably robust growth.

There are also many impressive success stories in emerging and developing economies and, most impressively perhaps, the former communist countries of Eastern Europe. They turned around their over-regulated countries with much unproductive public spending into quite successful countries with sustainable public finances.

4.2.5 The Political Economy of Consolidation and Reform

From an economic perspective, the case for timely consolidation and reform to avert a debt crisis seems quite compelling. The political costs of fiscal crisis are

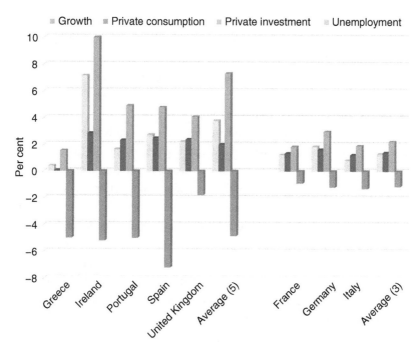

Figure 31 Economic dynamism: annual real economic, consumption and investment growth, change in unemployment rate, 2014–2017.
Source: OECD

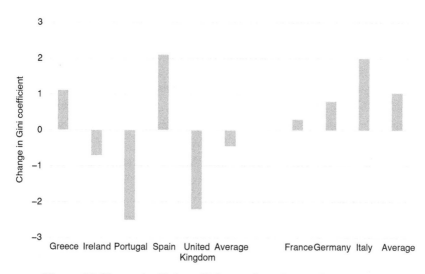

Figure 32 Change in Gini coefficient, selected countries, 2007–17
Source: OECD
Note: A negative change in the Gini coefficient implies a more equal income distribution.

also huge. Why, then, do countries not adapt in time? First, incumbent politicians fear that the costs of reform would be borne by them (via loss of support and re-election prospects) whereas the benefits would be reaped by their successors. Political costs may be particularly high if countries have to go to the IMF for support. However, Alesina et al. (2019) observe that this is not always true; there are good counter-examples.

The second reason could be an under-estimation of the probability and costs of fiscal crisis. Before the European fiscal crisis, governments did not have any experience with the vicious circle of fiscal, financial and competitive weakness that got Ireland and Spain into trouble even when public debt was rather low. Europe could have learnt from previous fixed exchange rate crises, as in Sweden in the 1990s or in Thailand around the turn of the millennium (see Jonung, Kiander and Vartia, 2009 for the Nordic crisis). But these experiences were not on the radar.

Third, euro area countries thought they were different from emerging economies so that destabilisation could not hit them. Europe did learn the hard way and created a regional, conditional support arrangement, the ESM, that combined solidarity with conditionality.

Fourth, countries were told they were safe by some influential economists, even if this only held under certain assumptions. Other voices warning of trouble were uncomfortable and not taken seriously. The influence of ideas is not to be under-estimated, especially if they are opportune and underpin certain interests. Fifth, countries may think that they will be saved by somebody else because they are too important to fail.

4.2.6 The Prospects for Scenario 1

There are good reasons to assume that many countries will not risk being hit by unsustainable debt and fiscal crisis – the economic and political costs are simply too high. Small countries, in particular, know that they are neither politically nor economically important enough to be saved without major conditionality. Indeed, IMF and EU projections underpin this expectation.

However, when looking at fiscal plans, the large advanced (and some emerging) countries seem to display neither ambition nor urgency. First, the largest countries may think that monetary independence and their safe-haven status will give them much more leeway for indebtedness, especially given the low real interest environment which they effectively control. Markets expect this regime to continue, so what is the urgency? Japan has been issuing more and more debt for a quarter of a century. Many observers still seem to believe that large countries are 'different', meaning a debt crisis is so distant and unlikely that the repercussions and huge costs are not worth considering.

The second argument applies to the euro area, where financial support has shifted from conditional IMF/ESM-based support in the early 2010s to almost unconditional support via European Central Bank (ECB) asset purchases and financial grants under NGEU. Although EU members agreed that NGEU was a one-off, expectations for further such schemes run high. This may create moral hazard, and countries may be tempted to delay reforms and seek further transfers in times of stress (Heinemann, 2021; Stark, 2021).

4.3 Scenario 2: Debt Workouts

4.3.1 Describing the Scenario

In the second scenario, countries with high public debt would decide not to pay and default. It sounds simple: you should pay X, but you decide not to do so. Instead, you either pay nothing or you agree with the creditor on how much you are really going to pay. But it is not that simple. The decision to default, and even the perceived risk thereof, sets in motion a complicated and drawn-out process. While this process aims at reaching a new agreement eventually, it sometimes takes years to reach it.

There are two main types of 'default'. The term 'debt workout' has started to be used because, legally, there is often no declaration of default (Roos, 2019; IMF, 2021e). The first is a so-called debt rescheduling. This does not change the need to repay the principle, that is the money lent. But it includes a delay in interest and amortisation payments to make the repayment easier. Interest payments are typically extended at the original rate (instead of higher prevailing market rates), which lightens the burden of the debt.

A so-called debt restructuring goes much further. It typically includes an explicit 'write-down' or 'forgiveness' of obligations. This can happen through a reduction in the face value of the debt (a 'haircut') or through contractually lowering the interest rate, or both. Restructurings are also referred to as 'debt-relief' or 'orderly defaults'.

In recent decades, there has been a tendency to reach negotiated solutions and avoid defaults. Eighty per cent of the countries that experienced sovereign debt crises before World War I declared default. This figure had declined to 20% by the start of the global financial crisis (Mitchener and Trebesch, 2021). In Europe, Greece defaulted while Ireland, Portugal and Spain did not.

4.3.2 The Process around Debt Workouts in an International Context

There are many kinds of debt. There is bond-based debt and bank debt, there is domestic debt and foreign debt, there is domestic currency debt and foreign currency debt, there is debt agreed on the basis of domestic law and foreign law. Domestic law-based debt is easier to default than foreign law-based debt because governments can change domestic laws.

There are more complications. For a workout, and depending on the contract, all or a majority of the creditors has to agree. In the case of bonded debt, this can involve many actors. As regards loans, there tend to be fewer banks involved, but to get them all at the table and in agreement is not an easy task either.

So-called collective action clauses (CACs) allow 'workouts' for bonded debt on the basis of less than unanimous agreement among creditors. This helps prevent the opportunistic opposition of some bondholders who hope to black-mail (i.e. sue) the government for a better deal. But the complex and fragmented creditor base remains a challenge, CACs only cover part of the outstanding stock of bonds, bank debt lacks restructuring provisions and often even the amount and conditions of all debt contracts is not known (Zettelmeyer, 2020; IMF 2020b).

Various formats and processes have been developed in the international sphere to minimise the financial, economic and political costs of a debt workout. Traditionally, the Paris Club brings together official creditors and debtors while the London Club co-ordinates private (bank) creditors. However, new formats are also emerging in the G20 context, given China's and other non-Western creditors' greater role in international debt. A 'common framework' has been agreed in 2020 for low-income countries (see G20, 2020; and related IMF and World Bank documents). This includes a commitment by all G20 and Paris Club creditors to co-ordinate and agree on 'key parameters' for 'timely and orderly debt treatment'.

There are tools and financial sweeteners that facilitate workouts. The debt sustainability analysis discussed in Section 2.5 is an integral part of inter-national negotiations. Workouts have to be part of a programme with the IMF, and in Europe, with the ESM to prevent moral hazard and ensure that the residual debt is paid.

4.3.3 Debt Workouts for Large Countries?

Arnold, Gulati and Panizza (2020) conducted an in-depth assessment of the legal and institutional obstacles to a debt workout for a large country, using the example of Italy. They argue that a workout would be possible and the proced-ural obstacles surmountable. They also argue that a more extensive use of CACs in bond contracts would be desirable to facilitate workouts.

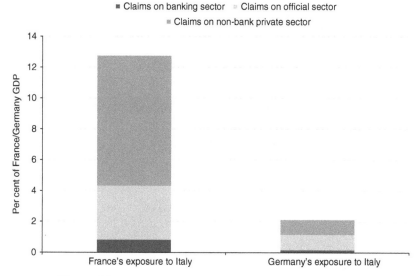

Figure 33 Exposure of France and Germany to Italy, 2020
Source: Bank for International Settlements

However, there are further obstacles. Cross-country exposure and the risk of contagion is particularly important when a large country gets into trouble. Some of Italy's neighbours, for example, are highly exposed to Italian debt through their financial system. In 2020, the exposure of France to Italy was 12.8% of French GDP (Figure 33). The French financial sector held about 4% of GDP or about 80 billion euros in Italian government debt. This is not much compared with the total stock of Italian debt and with French banks' balance sheets but it would be a huge loss relative to the French sector's capital. The exposure of German and other countries' banks is smaller but also quite significant. All in all, foreign investors held Italian government debt worth 48% of Italy's GDP in late 2020 (BIS). In addition, there is much controversy over the inter-central bank credit line 'Target' in the euro area where Bundesbank credits of over 1 trillion euros face corresponding debts, mainly by the Italian and Spanish central banks (see Sinn, 2014).

The biggest obstacles to orderly debt workouts for large countries relate to the bank–government 'doom loop'. Bank exposure to government debt is very high in Europe as concentration limits and risk weighting do not apply. This often makes government debt an attractive investment for banks. Italian banks, for example, held about 40% of GDP worth of Italian government debt on their balance sheet in 2020. At the bank level, this is very often a multiple of the bank's capital (Figure 34).

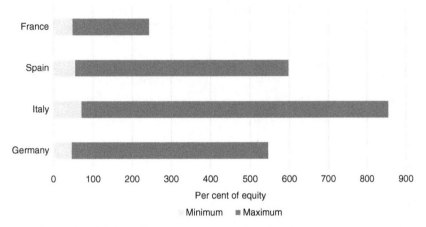

Figure 34 Holding of own government debt, 2016, per cent of equity, major banks

Source: European Banking Authority (2016)

A government debt crisis would, therefore, also imply a banking crisis because even modest losses from government debt would eat up banks' capital. A banking crisis, in turn, transmits losses to domestic and foreign investors. With the financial turmoil comes economic turmoil, within and across countries, potentially ricocheting back and forth. The larger the country and the more substantial the interconnectedness, the greater the potential for regional and global contagion.

Many proposals have been made, notably in Europe, to reduce the risk of a fiscal-financial 'doom loop'. They include a common deposit insurance that would reduce this risk at the price of more bank moral hazard. Codogno and van den Noord (2020, 2021) propose a substantial European debt issuance that satisfies banks' liquidity and funding needs while a hard upper limit on such common debt preserves governments' incentives to ensure fiscal soundness at home. However, none of this is so far 'in the making'.

The context and negative side effects of a workout in a very large country would, thus, be much more difficult to manage than for a small country. Arnold et al. (2020) may be right about the feasibility of large country debt workouts from a legal and procedural perspective. However, this is much more complicated to engineer and manage in an orderly manner from a financial and economic perspective, given the risk of unpredictable spillovers and spillbacks across countries.

4.3.4 Experiences with Defaults and 'Workouts'

Contrary to the claim of many economists, no debt is 'safe' as in 'risk-free', neither any private debt nor any public debt. Safe only means that there is a very low (but not zero) probability of default. The safest debt is rated

'AAA'. But the assessment of one bond does not look much at the 'bigger picture' where one bond's safety also depends on that of markets and countries as a whole.

The global financial crisis to a large extent originated from such a myopic view of debt that was only safe as long as a certain lax macro and regulatory environment prevailed and a tipping point had not been reached. As a result, even AAA debt defaulted in the US subprime crisis. And when these defaults accumulated to systemic proportions, they brought down many banks (including some of the largest), as well as several countries.

Global meltdowns are rare, and even the global financial crisis only qualifies partially. But the 1930s and earlier periods in history saw such meltdowns where large shares of government and private debt were 'non-performing'. Reinhart and Rogoff (2009) report that in the 1830s, the 1880s and the 1930s until after World War II, about 40–50% of all countries were in external default or restructuring. These episodes lasted a long time, often ten to fifteen years. Only a few countries never defaulted, as mentioned above.

Economically, debt workouts have almost always taken place in the context of financial and economic crisis. Countries experienced major declines of economic growth and also often major inflation (Reinhart and Rogoff, 2009; Mitchener and Trebesch, 2021). Adverse economic effects often persisted for a long time, even when they remained regional; the Latin American debt crisis is often described as the continent's 'lost decade'. However, there is often no way around workouts and they can be very successful when they breathe new life into affected countries. Ultimately, growth and opportunities recovered in Latin America, Africa and elsewhere.

4.3.5 A 'Workout' for Greece

The Greece workout is worth looking at. The Greek drama started with the discovery of hugely under-reported fiscal imbalances (Papaconstantinou, 2016). After a drawn-out period of confidence loss, adjustment programmes and back-and-forth negotiations, Greece and its creditors undertook a major debt workout in March and April 2012. It involved over 200 billion euros plus some state-owned enterprise debt – over 100% of GDP in total. The face-value debt decline was 107 billion euros or 52% of GDP, and the net-present-value decline was about 60%, one of the harshest haircuts for a middle-income country ever (Zettelmeyer et al., 2013).

The restructuring was economically reasonable and successful. It could have been done earlier, with more relief, and with a less generous treatment of the hold-outs and the ECB who were both paid in full (Zettelmeyer, et al., 2013).

Contrary to fears and claims in the run-up to the workout, there were very limited spillovers to other vulnerable countries, as these had already been ring-fenced in separate support programmes. This illustrates the importance of timely action, as part of strong and workable procedures, the availability of large safety nets and the willingness of governments and creditors to collaborate.

4.3.6 The Political Economy of Debt Workouts

The group of proponents of debt workouts has been growing, notably as regards highly indebted developing and emerging economies (IMF and World Bank). The interest of target countries has been limited, arguably for reputational reasons and to maintain market access. Only a few small and very poor countries have pursued this avenue as of 2020. This points to important political economy challenges where it is again worth distinguishing between small and large countries.

Creditors and debtors have an interest in finding a negotiated solution in a debt workout, if such a workout cannot be avoided and if that enhances the economic prospects of the country and the repayment prospects for the creditor. Large banks and asset managers have an incentive to co-operate when the client country is small and/or poor, as adverse reputational effects are likely to outweigh the additional financial gains from taking a tougher line.

On the side of small countries, the 'workout' period typically involves financial difficulties but they would be potentially more severe without a solution. The required IMF/World Bank programme is politically costly but international support programmes also provide financial sweeteners and under-pin the durability of a deal. They help minimise losses while also mitigating contagion risks. Therefore, it is mainly small countries that have taken this route in the past and are likely to do so in the future. Support and reforms promise to boost growth and re-establish fiscal sustainability, which enhances policy makers' popularity post workout.

For European countries, though, the incentive structure may be somewhat different. There is no scope for a supportive devaluation within the euro area, the tumultuous Greek debt restructuring and its political ramifications deter any repetition (despite its economic and financial success), and there will probably also be the hope for financial support from European partners – many of whom would not want a repeat of the 'Greece' experience and its risk of contagion.

Large countries are likely to be rather uninterested in debt workouts from a political economy perspective. For these countries, the political 'humiliation' costs would be even greater than for smaller ones. Conditionality imposed as part of a rescue programme would lack credibility. Moreover, the management of workouts would be very difficult and the economic fallout at home and abroad would be much greater. The existing procedures are not designed for large countries. In Europe, it would raise the question of euro membership which, in turn, would further exacerbate instability, spillovers and spillbacks. The size of international financial safety nets is likely to be too small for large countries (see Section 3.5). Other governments, if not the global community, would fear potential broader global ramifications, including on their own economies and debt.

4.4 Scenario 3: Debt Reduction via Financial Repression

4.4.1 Describing the Scenario

The third scenario relies on moderate inflation in conjunction with negative real interest rates. This is also called financial repression. If inflation is positive and the financing costs for government are lower or even around zero, the real value of public debt declines. This is the case at the time of writing in the euro area, the United Kingdom and the United States.

The debt-deflation effect of financial repression is illustrated in Figure 35 for a starting debt level of 100% of GDP. A combination of 1% inflation and zero interest rates reduces the real value of debt by almost 10% in a decade and by almost 30% in one generation or thirty-five years. A persistent inflation rate of 2% halves the real value of debt in one generation. Higher inflation than 2% implies an even greater effect.

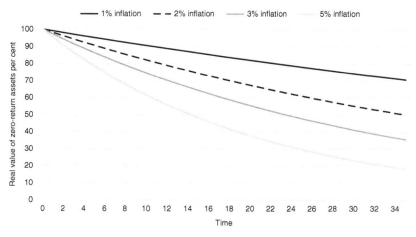

Figure 35 Effect of inflation on the real value of zero-return assets
Source: Own calculations

The financial repression effect is, hence, significant but it is working slowly. It is no surprise that it features prominently in the relaxed approach to public debt of many economists (and politicians). If real interest rates stay significantly negative for a very long time, there seems indeed no urgency for bringing debt down; there even seems to be room for more debt.

Note, however, that there is a flip side. The price level doubles in a generation. As every debtor has a creditor, the real value of the money and government bonds also halve in a generation and this hurts mainly the wealth and income prospects of the middle classes who hold such debt in their account or in their pension funds. Paul Volcker, the former Federal Reserve Chairman, asks about the 'purpose, and for that matter morality, of ... deliberately debasing the nation's currency a little every year' (Volcker and Harper, 2018).

Moreover, there is an important precondition for this scenario to work. Real financing costs must not adjust to inflation, or at least not by much and not fast. Higher financing costs reduce and may even over-compensate for the debt-deflating effect of inflation. This effect is simulated in Figure 36, again on the basis of 100% of GDP of public debt. The figure assumes a starting inflation of 3% and 0% interest rates in t1. The refinancing need is 20% of the debt stock every year. In t2, refinancing costs rise from 0 to 3%. This has to be paid on 20% of the debt in t2, on 40% in t3 and so on. With rising interest expenditure, the debt-deflating effect shrinks. By the sixth year, when the whole debt stock has been refinanced, the net effect on the real value of debt is zero. The total gain from inflation and financial repression is the integral under the net-gains line,

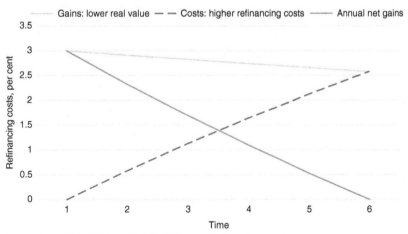

Assumption: 100% of GDP public debt, 20% annual refinancing needs

Figure 36 The transitory benefits of repression (3% higher inflation, 3% higher refinancing costs)

Source: Own calculations

which in this case is roughly 9% of GDP – and very much less than it would have been without the financing cost increase. Lower inflation or higher interest rates would imply even smaller gains. A slower refinancing process would mean more reduction in the real value of public debt and vice versa.

The literature argues that future gains from financial repression would be significant but still limited. Hilscher et al. (2014) see scope for a reduction by 4–23% of GDP depending on the durability of low interest rates and repression (see also Aizenman and Marion, 2011). Krause and Moyen (2016) also argue that only very long-lasting repression will make a significant impact of up to at most 30% of GDP.

Based on forward interest rates in markets, the ten-year fiscal projections of the European Commission (2021) discussed in Section 2.5 assume a significant contribution from inflation to eroding the real value of public debt. This amounts to some 15% of GDP over a decade which, however, is largely compensated by continuing deficits.

There is another precondition. The stability of financial repression over long periods of time requires the persistence of confidence. There has to be confidence that inflation does not rise beyond what has been promised or investors will ask for higher returns. This requires a sufficiently competent handling of economic, fiscal, financial and monetary challenges to maintain such confidence. Otherwise, financial repression will not be stable and loss of confidence and rising inflation could mutate into destabilisation (see Section 4.5). The more and the longer inflation deviates from the original 'promise' (which in most countries is 2%), the larger the potential debt-reducing effect – but the larger also the risk of losing credibility and confidence.

4.4.2 Other Measures to Underpin the Persistence of Repression

Governments can underpin favourable financing conditions by a number of additional preventive and reactive measures. Governments have created insurance and safety net schemes (see Section 3.5). Foreign currency reserves can help stabilise the exchange rate and domestic financing conditions. Support from the IMF and multilateral development banks can boost stability. Liquidity provision via central banks' swap and repo lines can also stabilise financing costs. Asset purchases by central banks aim to lower financing costs of bond issuers including governments. Havlik et al. (2021) found a significant effect on interest rate spreads after the announcement of the ECB's new purchase programme, PEPP, in spring 2020.

In Europe, many observers expect not only continued central bank action but also a repetition of the NGEU common debt issuance in the next crisis. The expectation of growing debt mutualisation will keep risk spreads low so that high-debt countries can continue benefitting from low interest rates (and financial repression). At the same time, moral hazard may increase overall indebtedness and its perceived riskiness in the euro area. Maintaining confidence and preventing moral hazard in fiscal policies remains key to containing debt and preventing a euro debt crisis in lieu of national ones in the long run. This is what the Stability and Growth Pact was meant to do but its implementation has been deficient (Schuknecht et al., 2011 and many others).

Finally, financial repression can be underpinned by domestic and international controls. Rajan and Zingales (2003/2018) argue that in the face of crisis and adversity, 'popular revulsions and special interests' call for the taming of volatile prices and financial markets. This can include more or less 'subtle' measures: (1) price controls on rents, consumer goods and administrative prices to limit measured inflation, (2) prohibition of the ownership of foreign bank accounts, currency and even gold to prevent capital flight and 'speculation', (3) controls of interest rates, preferential government access to low-cost financing and forced lending to ensure low debt-servicing costs, (4) different types of wealth taxes, (5) digital central bank money to employ more negative interest rates, (6) various forms and degrees of capital controls on outflows from crisis countries and inflows into safe-haven countries to prevent 'speculation' and confidence loss turning into capital flight, (7) many forms of obstacles via tax and administrative rules. All of these provisions have been employed at some point in the past. Capital controls have been relabelled 'capital flow management measures' as part of the 'macro-prudential toolkit' to sound less damaging and threatening.

A far-reaching implementation of this non-exhaustive list would fundamentally change our economic and financial policy regime back into a much more controlled, special-interest-dominated and arbitrary world. However, it would enhance the chances of continuing financial repression beyond its 'sell-by date' in an open, global economy.

4.4.3 Experiences with Financial Repression

Financial repression was used quite successfully in a number of historical episodes. After World War II and until the 1960s, high economic growth and moderate inflation in a modest interest rate environment helped bring down public debt rapidly. However, it is often forgotten that this also involved broadly balanced budgets over extended periods of time in most countries. The Bretton Woods system provided a US-backed and gold-based anchor for the monetary system. Moreover, widespread capital controls and a significant amount of non-market-based monetary and financial policy instruments, such as directed credits and quantitative credit controls, significantly slowed down market reactions to imbalances and thus kept the monetary order stable for a long time.

The financial repression effect in debt reduction was significant but not huge. Reinhart and Sbrancia (2015) found an average effect of 8% of GDP for twelve countries during the 1945 to 1956 period. However, in the later Bretton Woods period and during the 1970s, the dynamic changed. Rising inflation devalued the stock of 'old debt' but new debt faced rising nominal and real interest rates so that the financial repression effect disappeared. Countries had overstretched their room for policy manoeuvre and, with that, lost confidence and control.

It is also interesting to look at the past twenty-five years when price stability prevailed. Japan is often seen as the master of financial repression. But it is not clear whether that is a correct perception. The Japanese consumer price inflation index stood at 100 in 1999, at 100 in 2016 and at 101.8 in 2020. Inflation was zero over twenty years but interest rates were also zero or slightly positive. The financial repression effect was, therefore, zero. Low growth and persistent high deficits drove Japan's debt to 256% of GDP by 2020.

The United Kingdom and the United States contracted new debt at negative real interest rates in the post-global financial crisis period. As a result, their governments benefitted from a debt-reducing effect to the order of 7% of GDP after the global financial crisis – that is, 1–2% of GDP per annum (Reinhart and Sbrancia, 2015). In Italy (which does not have its own monetary policy), effective interest rates on government debt were on average markedly higher than inflation and nominal GDP growth. Hence, inflation had a moderate debt-reducing effect in several high-credibility countries but no such effect occurred where debt was very high.

4.4.4 Political Economy of Financial Repression

From a political economy perspective, the financial repression scenario looks quite attractive. For short-term–oriented policy makers, it is likely to trump politically costly reform or debt restructuring (scenarios 1 and 2), especially if the expectation is that low real interest rates will continue for a long time. Still, governments should have enough of an incentive to avoid major policy errors so as to maintain reasonable stability prospects, confidence and control. This incentive should be strongest for large countries, where a fiscal crisis would almost certainly lead to major turmoil at home and to spillovers to and spill-backs from abroad.

If miscalculations, major external shocks, policy errors and excessive short termism are avoided, financial repression can, thus, continue for a long time.

What is the likelihood? Many economists assume that the likelihood is 100%. The big fiscal and financial crisis that some hawks predicted never came, and why should it come any time soon? In the past decade, politicians have always found a solution, even if only temporarily. Politics, not markets, should determine how long the music plays. Political economy incentives suggest that indeed, policy makers will do everything to make the good times last as long as possible.

Central banks are in an ambiguous position. When debt is not yet too high, and fiscal dominance is still avoidable, they will want to maintain their credibility. This will help the durability of this scenario. But the speed and magnitude of financial market reactions in the global financial crisis, the 'taper tantrum' of 2013 and the 2020 'dash for cash' have made it more difficult for central banks to assert themselves. Central banks (and fiscal authorities) must be congratulated for their handling of the global financial crisis and the pandemic. Nevertheless, the verdict is still out on the long-term effects and the persistence of the 2021/22 inflation acceleration. The impact on moral hazard, debt and risk accumulates over time. This has not made the job of central bankers easier looking forward.

All in all, there is a significant probability that policy makers in many countries and especially in the large, advanced ones will continue to rely on financial repression to contain debt dynamics. This can continue for a long time and, hopefully, long enough that consolidation and reform can restore sustainability. Still, there is a risk that this scenario is not stable and becomes very unpleasant when confidence is lost.

4.5 Scenario 4: A Risk Scenario of Destabilisation

4.5.1 Describing the Scenario

The most undesirable scenario going forward is that of destabilisation due to a loss of confidence. This is expecially concerning when it occurs in large countries. A continuation of financial repression alone is not likely to bring public debt down to safe levels within even a decade when the starting level is 120% or 150% of GDP. Chances are that, at some point, financing conditions worsen, a further major shock occurs and/or policy errors are made.

How can the loss of confidence and stability come about and what would that process look like in the future? The previous sections discussed the 'inputs': high debt and fiscal risks are the basis. This alone can be enough to trigger a confidence crisis, as experienced by Greece when the true extent of its imbalances was revealed. Financing costs for governments rise and market access might halt completely. Additional risk factors are increasing spending prospects, lower growth, private financial imbalances, which are compounded by rising inflation, real interest rates and risk spreads. These factors can set in motion a vicious circle of worsening confidence and economic, financial and fiscal instability.

It is important to note that this destabilisation scenario can come about with or without inflation. Moreover, it can be at first deflationary before turning inflationary. If the massive asset price boom of the past decade turned into 'bust' when financing costs rose, this would be destabilising and deflationary, as in the global financial crisis. However, if this 'bust' came together with high public debt, growing public discontent, demands for wages, further fiscal expansion, capital flight and currency crisis, it could also well become inflationary (or stagflationary), as it did in other crises in the past. Another global supply shock of the oil crisis type (e.g., potentially the war in Ukraine?), a closure of important shipping routes, persistent skill shortages, a major global drought, a protectionist 'wave' – such events and policy errors could contribute to igniting inflationary dynamics.

4.5.2 The Role of Different Policy Actors in This Scenario

If and how a destabilisation scenario unfolds hinges on the starting point, but also on the strength of institutions and the behaviour of policy actors, including social partners, fiscal authorities and central banks. We mentioned the starting point of outright confidence loss in governments' fiscal sustainability. Alternatively, rising inflation in a high-debt country can be the starting point, for example due to continued monetary and fiscal expansion, wage pressures or supply disturbances. This is graphically represented in Figure 37, in moving from step i) to steps ii) and iii).

In such a situation, central banks have the option of tightening their policies. If they decide not to tighten (or not enough), they signal that they are willing to compromise their mandate to protect governments and an over-exposed financial industry – fiscal and financial dominance are 'at work'. In Figure 37 this is reflected by the upper path A, leading to steps iv) and v). It signals to governments, social partners and financial players that they can continue with reckless behaviour because the central bank will bail them out. Inflation expectations are likely to adjust, and long-term rates rise (step vi).

Once on this path, central banks are likely to remain behind the curve as political and special interest pressure continues. At some point, confidence wanes (step vii). Capital flight sets in, a currency crisis emerges, and inflation accelerates further. Financial repression mutates into stagflation and destabilisation (step viii).

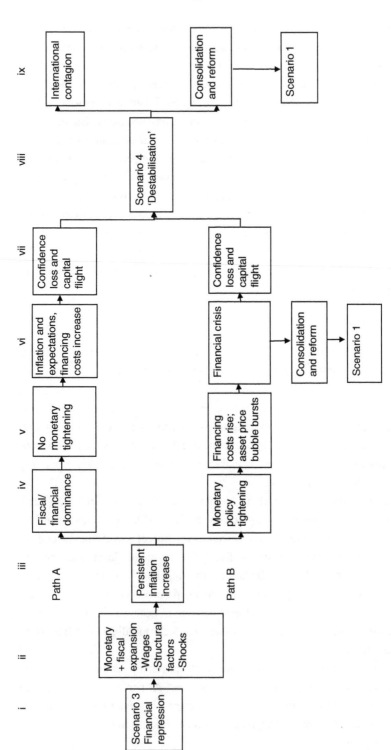

Figure 37 From financial repression to destabilisation

The second path is also not without risks (lower path B in Figure 37). If central banks tighten monetary policy, they signal 'monetary dominance', that is they are not willing to compromise their mandate (step iv). If asset prices, debt and financial risks are very high, tighter monetary policies may lead to a crash in asset prices (step v) and into a financial crisis with doubts about the safety of government debt (step vi), as happened during the global financial crisis. Countries then have to undertake consolidation and reforms to maintain confidence. De facto, this means behaving like in Scenario 1 (Section 4.2). Without reform efforts, confidence would be lost, and capital flight and a currency crisis would occur. This, in turn, would stoke inflation as it did in many such crises in the past (step vii). In other words, a (deflationary) financial crisis would then become inflationary and end in destabilisation as well (step viii). If imbalances and risks are too large, central banks may be in a situation where they cannot win.

4.5.3 International Repercussions

From a 'traditional' perspective, many would argue that the story should end here with the necessary adjustment and reform (step ix), moving to the equivalent of Scenario 1. This is what many emerging and developing countries did in the past, typically with IMF assistance. Some such crises implied contagion and resulted in more adjustment programmes in the region while global repercussions remained limited.

However, the most 'interesting' part of this discussion is perhaps just starting with the question, how significant is the potential for contagion (step ix)? The Latin American, the Asian and the European crises were in fact signalling a growing degree of regional turbulence and contagion as more important economies became involved. Moreover, previous crises were mainly banking crises and, while banking stability has improved, the March 2020 turmoil shows the growing instability risks from a run-prone non-bank financial sector (see Section 3.5).

If a large, advanced country were to move towards destabilisation, it would have graver repercussions. Such a development might well trigger a broader reassessment of global financial risks and risk prices. Global capital could start 'sloshing' around in search for safety. Countries might decide to reallocate reserves across currencies. Central bank swap and repo lines might be needed more than ever while their availability for problem countries might become more restricted. Contagion might 'produce' two groups of countries, the safe and the unsafe. And the two groups may not be stable: countries that were seen as safe at the beginning may not stay safe as the turmoil unfolds and spreads.

Pressure for capital controls and possibly trade protection will mount, with further adverse consequences.

Such a scenario could also trigger a scramble for financial support. Global and regional policy coordination and financial safety nets could reach their limits. For individual G7 countries, two years' worth of government financing needs (40–50% of GDP) could reach US$ 1 trillion and more. The IMF could be requested to issue SDR on a large scale and thereby become a kind of global ATM. However, the dynamics of such a scenario would remain highly uncertain, given very high debt and, thus, contagion risks in almost all large economies.

In fact, this is the main difference today compared with the global financial and European crises: at that time, financial support could be built on the reasonably healthy balance sheets of the largest countries, both via the IMF and via new European mechanisms. These are only some, very speculative considerations but they illustrate how complex and far-reaching the repercussions of a confidence loss might be.

4.5.4 Experiences with Destabilisation: Lessons and Differences from the 1970s

For those who are not convinced that this is a possible scenario, it is worthwhile looking back to the 1970s and its run-up. At that time, advanced countries experienced several of the adverse factors and surprises referred to above and in Section 3. Fiscal policies were very expansionary as expenditure ratios rose and slowing growth prospects were not anticipated. Wage increases were above levels consistent with price stability and the money overhang of the 1960s became more inflationary once the Bretton Woods system's gold anchor was lost. Adverse supply side factors – industrial policy and market regulation – contributed to low growth and inflation. Two oil crises stoked inflation and stagflation. International capital flows and trade integration, however, were still quite limited.

The upper path (A) in Figure 37 describes rather well what happened in slow motion in the 1970s: expansionary policies at the outset fanning inflation, with central banks and election-oriented fiscal policy makers increasingly falling 'behind the curve'. A de-anchoring of inflation expectations gradually set in (ECB, 2010). This affected the largest countries just as much as the smaller ones.

It is worth commenting a bit more on the experiences of the USA and the UK. The UK had lost its status as lead global financial player with World War II when the US dollar overtook the pound as the most important reserve currency (Figure 38). Until the late 1960s, however, about 30% of global reserves were still held in British pounds. By the mid-1970s, this share had declined to near

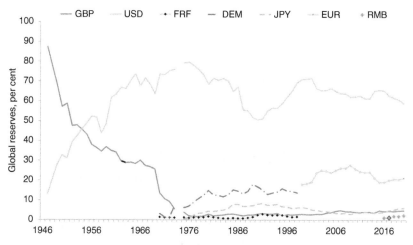

Figure 38 Currency composition of globally disclosed foreign exchange
reserves: 1946–2020
Source: ECB, updated from Eichengreen et al. (2017)

zero, as the international community lost faith. Pound divestment contributed to
the exchange rate decline and the inflationary burst in the UK. Interest rates on
government bonds shot up to 15–25% in 1974/75 with inflation of around 15%
(Figure 39a). As mentioned, in the summer of 1976, the UK got a loan from the
G10 and then, in the winter, from the IMF. The then Bank of England Chief
Economist Christopher Dow describes the situation in his memoirs (2013) as
'out of control' with 'collective hysteria'.

The crisis took longer to develop in the United States. Despite confidence
problems in the early 1970s, with rising inflation and major non-market interventions in the economy, the US dollar first took over much of the international
reserve space of the pound (Figure 38). The Japanese Yen and the German Mark
played a growing role thereafter and the dollar share gradually fell. Inflation
showed a peak in both oil crises but monetary policies reacted late and real
interest rates turned negative (Figure 39b). In the late 1970s, confidence col-
lapsed and the dollar depreciated strongly. Paul Volcker (Feldstein 2013 and
Volcker 2018) commented that 'the whole international exchange rate situation
got out of hand' with a 'currency crisis' and a 'run on the dollar'. Homer and
Sylla (1991) reported that 'an atmosphere of crisis pervaded markets'.

Germany and Switzerland, by contrast, managed monetary policies more
prudently, which exerted a restraining effect on fiscal and wage policies. They
maintained positive real interest rates (Figure 39c for Germany). This underpinned the role and strength of their currencies and it started the 'Siegeszug', the
triumph of independent central banks.

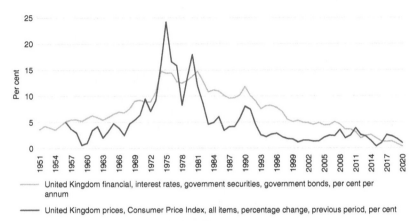

Figure 39a United Kingdom: inflation and short-term government
financing rate

Source: IMF and World Bank

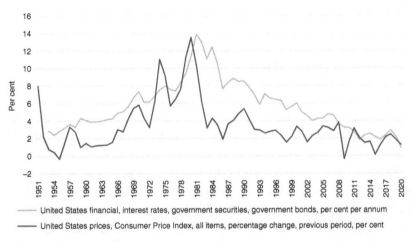

Figure 39b United States: inflation and short-term government financing rate
Source: IMF and World Bank

With the change of hands in the Federal Reserve to Paul Volcker and to pro-market governments in the USA and UK, monetary policy credibility and financial calm were restored. This came with very high real interest rates for governments before confidence came back and inflation went down. The United States resumed its role as global economic leader and the UK reinvented itself as a strong global financial player.

However, it is important to note the differences between the experiences then and in the 2010s and early 2020s. The European fiscal crisis involved rather small economies, whereas the 'drama' of the 1970s was mainly around some

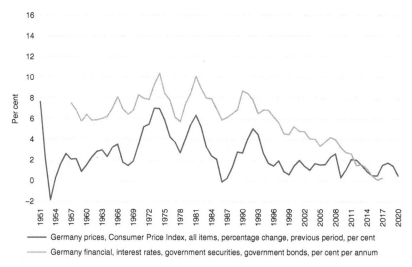

Figure 39c Germany: inflation and short-term government financing rate
Source: IMF and World Bank

large, advanced countries. But most importantly, capital markets were rather closed forty years ago so that capital flows did not much exacerbate the confidence crisis. If the European crisis of the 2010s had involved the largest advanced and emerging countries, things would have probably unfolded even more dramatically.

It is also important to look at the implications for emerging economies. In the late 1970s, 'cheap' money was recycled to Latin America and created huge mal-investments and turbulence there. There are concerns that some countries are quite vulnerable again, given rising debt in the global low interest environment (IMF, 2021c, d). At the same time, things are different. There is much more local currency finance, and indebtedness is mostly lower than in advanced countries. Already in the global financial crisis, many emerging economies were on the 'safe' side of contagion. Emerging countries with sound finances should find themselves relatively well placed in future turmoil.

4.5.5 Political Economy of Debt Reduction via Destabilisation

There are important lessons from the 1970s for today from a political economy perspective. The dynamics of destabilisation following opportunistic policy making by social partners, central banks and treasuries at that time seems a far cry from the environment prevailing in the early 2020s. However, there are at least some early warning signs. Special interests in industry will want to ride the wave of re-nationalisation, climate change and other reasons to attain privileges –

this is not good for growth. Labour seems to discover its much-increased bargaining power, according to some indicators. Both factors are inflationary. There is no political, financial or academic pressure on fiscal authorities to take a cautious approach, while debt and spending pressures are rising further. Asset price bubbles seem to be prevalent. Real (equilibrium) interest rates may gradually rise again. With record public debt and significant financial vulnerabilities, interest rate increases might be difficult to absorb. Should there be signs of financial pressures, governments will leave no stone unturned before they undertake unpopular reforms or seek international support, including asking central banks to buy them more time.

Central banks are much more independent today than in the 1970s or at any time in history. Hence, there is no compelling reason for delayed action. But they are operating in a very difficult environment. They will be tempted to move late if there is a risk that they could be blamed for an early move causing stress and crisis. This is probably more the case today than in the 1970s, when governments had more time to react to signs of instability. As mentioned in Section 3.4, central bank balance sheets contain much government debt so that interest rate increases would affect their financial situation. Central banks could, thus, again face pressure to delay action should inflation accelerate.

All in all, there is a chance that negative (or very low) real interest rates will continue for some time. This will help reduce debt and buy time for reform. However, there is also a non-negligible risk that the ongoing financial repression scenario is not stable and that adverse debt, inflation and financing cost dynamics re-develop for political economy reasons (see Mayer and Schnabl, 2021). This would be reasonably manageable if it affected only small advanced or emerging economies. However, the fiscal outlook is most vulnerable in the largest countries.

5 Conclusions

> Crises have blown up because the rules of the social market [economy] have not been observed.
>
> (Angela Merkel, May 2013; quoted in MacKenzie 2013)

Private debt has been 'on record' for 7,000 years, public debt for about 2,500 years. The first laws and regulations around debt emerged almost 4,000 years ago in Babylon, and the first debt crises in Greece and the Roman Empire gave rise to frameworks that still influence our approach to debt today (Homer and Sylla, 1991). Government debt has had a very chequered record since antiquity. It has been everything but safe and often less safe than private debt.

The perception of government debt being safe has, therefore, been a great achievement. Starting perhaps with the United Kingdom a few centuries ago, it became 'the rule' in advanced countries only after World War II. A lot of progress has been built on it: a smooth operation of government in producing high-quality services, credible social security systems, well-functioning financial markets, price stability and international economic openness (Eichengreen et al., 2021). It has emerged on the basis of strong institutions that created trust and confidence between the most different and remote people. This is a remarkable human achievement that it would be a tragedy to lose.

Public finance sustainability, however, is at risk post COVID, especially in some of the largest countries. Public debt has reached record levels equivalent to those prevailing after World War II and there is no meaningful decline in sight. Moreover, there are huge additional fiscal risks from population ageing and financial crisis. The costs of climate change and of geopolitical challenges may also weigh on fiscal sustainability. These risks are confirmed in well-accepted international sustainability analysis for many countries. However, the global dimension is under-appreciated: high-debt and high-risk countries comprise over 45% if not 60% of the global economy and include the largest ones.

There are additional risk factors that are not always on the radar screen. Public spending post COVID is very high, often too high to be financeable and often unproductive, while pressures for even more spending mount. Long-term growth prospects may well be lower than predicted amidst major financial distortions, asset price booms and moral hazard, and inflation may increase more persistently than expected while real interest rates may also rise again. This could further burden confidence in the sustainability of public finances, in tandem with a decline of trust in our fiscal and monetary institutions. International interdependence would increase the speed at which confidence loss can occur and exacerbate the international fallout while potentially stoking financial and economic protectionism.

If these facts and the analysis are not convincing, and more spending and more debt are seen as the better option, there is no need for change. Otherwise, they are a compelling reason to bring debt and fiscal risks down. Given that a meaningful debt reduction takes a long time (success stories show a debt decline by 20–30% of GDP in ten to fifteen years), this should start sooner rather than later.

How can this come about? The first, and best scenario would be ambitious fiscal consolidation as part of a comprehensive, medium-term reform package. Many countries have successfully followed this path in the past, seeking better rather than more spending. But while many small countries are expected to do so quietly and responsibly in the future, there seems to be little appetite for it, especially amongst the larger ones.

In history, the alternative to paying off debt was often rather drastic: self-enslavement and prison for individuals, and embargos and military intrusion for governments. Those days are fortunately long gone. Countries can seek a debt workout and negotiate a reduction in their debt burden in return for the promise to pay the rest, underpinned by conditionality and international monitoring. This has worked for many smaller countries in the past, including Greece, but it has been politically costly. Large countries, in particular, will find this scenario quite undesirable.

The third scenario involves negative real interest rates that erode the real value of public debt via financial repression. Many advanced countries are in that situation in the early 2020s. Financial repression allows a gradual debt reduction if the inflation effect is not countervailed by higher spending and deficits and higher financing costs. Moderate debt reductions have been achieved this way in the past. Such a scenario is far from ideal as it tends to hurt growth and opportunities. But it is also far from the worst as it maintains order and buys time for reforms.

However, it should not be taken for granted that this scenario is stable 'forever'. High debt at tipping points, rising inflation and financing costs, domestic policy errors and external shocks can stoke confidence loss, crisis and destabilisation. The 1970s were a prominent episode for this fourth, risk scenario. At the time, confidence crises affected even the UK and the USA. But in a world of capital controls, everything happened much more slowly than it would today. The crises in Asia and Europe since the late 1990s are indicative of growing international spillovers, and the 'dash for cash' in March 2020 was perhaps the fastest 'sudden stop' ever. If this were to happen to one (or several) of the largest economies, financial inter-dependence might well lead to rather dramatic spillover and spillback effects where the re-introduction of capital (and trade) controls might further stoke rather than contain the turmoil.

5.1 The Scenarios: Who Benefits and Who Gets Hurt?

The post-COVID high-debt environment also reflects the growing influence of vocal and influential interest groups that gain distributional advantages at the expense of society and sustainability. It is hard to find another explanation for the strong and debt-financed expansion of ageing-related spending in recent decades. It is hard to forward a different explanation for various financial bailouts, even well after the global financial crisis (and against the promise of never making taxpayers pay again). In March 2020, many analysts observed that the much-rumoured 'central bank put' had been extended to the influential non-bank and wealth-management sector in the 'dash for cash'. Those who invested huge fortunes in stocks, bonds and real estate must have been quite satisfied.

By contrast, some observers try to discredit consolidation and reforms of government as 'evil austerity' that hurts in particular the vulnerable. This does not correspond with the facts, as the literature on such experiences shows. It is true that consolidation will require governments to look at excessive spending and benefits and to become more effective. But in fact, vulnerable groups profit most from the resulting virtuous cycle of better spending, more employment, greater opportunities and higher incomes. Fiscal sustainability will make social security systems more reliable and decarbonisation more credible. This again benefits the poor disproportionately. Consolidation and reform will also allow a normalisation of monetary policies and asset values, which underpins the value of the savings of the poor and middle classes. Maintaining fiscal sustainability is, therefore, the most social and socially sustainable scenario.

The distributional implications of debt workouts have their negative and positive aspects. The turmoil around such workouts undermines jobs and investment, which, in turn, hurts the poor and vulnerable most. But the prospect of less debt and successful reform will also benefit them. The losses from debt reduction will affect creditors adversely but they often have already been compensated via higher interest rates.

It is not surprising that there is little opposition to financial repression. First, it is quite problematic from a distributional perspective. It is a 'stealth' tax on the money-holding class that puts their savings in bank accounts or in bonds and, as mentioned, these are the middle- and lower-middle-income people. But the same people profit from the protected income and jobs during a crisis. The well-off who are invested in inflation-hedged assets get away lightly. Second, in the longer term, lower growth with lower incomes and fewer opportunities hurts 'normal' people more. But the costs and benefits are well hidden and those who pay are quite dispersed, which is no good lobbying-base. Hence, although financial repression is not desirable, we can and will have to live with it and hope that it can build a bridge to consolidation and reform in the not too distant future.

Destabilisation is the worst scenario from both an economic and a distributional perspective. Destabilisation hurts everybody. While the well-informed and well-off will shift their assets to (increasingly illusive) safety, 'normal people' are likely to stay put and lose out. The loss of jobs and savings will hurt the poor and vulnerable the most. Economic and financial turmoil will stoke societal divisions. Populists will blame the failed establishment and meritocracy. The re-introduction of controls and protectionism will reduce our economic freedom and fuel international conflicts.

There is a good chance that this scenario will not happen. If it does happen, some kind of order will be restored afterwards, as was done in the past. All may be well afterwards if we take the right action and re-strengthen our policies and institutions. But chances are that the fallout in between will be serious, and we might not quite get back the order that we have learnt to appreciate. All this speaks for more fiscal prudence going forward.

Epilogue

As this Element was about to go to print, the war in Ukraine broke out. If this conflict were to be relatively short-lived and the durable implications for trade, financing costs, growth and public finances limited, the additional challenge for fiscal sustainability will also be contained. At the same time, the conflict – just like the COVID-19 pandemic before – showed yet again that there are always going to be adverse fiscal surprises that countries will need to expect and to have buffers for on top of those that are already well known.

Moreover, there are good reasons to believe that the war will reinforce the challenges that were already becoming apparent beforehand: inflation dynamics may accelerate even more durably than expected, and affect wage dynamics as well. Supply chain disruptions and decoupling are likely to go further than anticipated earlier with adverse consequences for productivity, cost and growth prospects. All these factors are negatives for public debt sustainability. If the war continues for long, and related economic and financial measures significantly disrupt the global economy, fiscal crises become more likely.

It is natural that policy makers try to calm the population about risks ahead and not portray the trade-offs between spending on one or the other challenge too starkly. However, if anything, these developments have strengthened the case for prudent fiscal and financial management with the emphasis on high-quality, priority spending and growth-friendly reform going forward. Such an approach will help avoid the less desirable scenarios of default, durable financial repression or even destabilization, and, instead, maintain debt sustainability, especially in the world's large economies.

Annex Table Country data, gross public debt, deficit and expenditure, household and corporate debt, per cent of GDP

Advanced countries	Gross public debt	Overall balance	Public expenditure	Household debt	Corporate debt	Emerging economies	Gross public debt	Overall balance	Public expenditure	Household debt	Corporate debt
	2020	2020	2020	2020	2020		2020	2020	2020	2020	2020
Average	120.1	−11.7	47.4	77.1	101.1	Average	64.4	−9.8	35.0	46.6	101.7
Euro Area	96.9	−7.6	54.1	62.7		Asia	67.6	−10.8	34.4		
G7	136.7	−13.2	48.9			Europe	37.6	−5.9	40.2		
G20 Advanced	130.8	−12.7	47.9			Latin America	77.7	−8.8	34.6		
Australia	63.1	−9.9	45.0	123.5	72.2	MENAP	56.6	−9.9	33.7		
Austria	85.2	−9.6	57.9	53.2	99.8	G20 Emerging	65.6	−10.4	35.7		
Belgium	115.0	−10.2	60.8	67.7	166	Algeria	53.1	−7.7	38.0		
Canada[1]	117.8	−10.7	52.4	112.2	132.4	Angola	127.1	−1.7	19.9		
Cyprus	118.2	−5.0	47.4			Argentina	103.0	−8.9	41.6	5.6	19.3
Czech Republic	37.6	−5.9	47.9	34.0	57.2	Belarus	48.0	−3.3	38.4		
Denmark	43.4	−3.5	55.1	111.9	136.5	Brazil	98.9	−13.4	42.7	36.9	54
Estonia	18.5	−5.4	44.7			Bulgaria	23.8	−3.0	38.8		
Finland	67.1	−4.8	56.7	69.3	123	Chile	32.5	−7.1	29.0	48.2	115.9
France	113.5	−9.9	62.4	68.7	171.1	China	66.8	−11.4	37.0	61.7	160.7

Country					
Germany	68.9	-4.2	51.1	58.8	73.2
Greece	213.1	-9.9	58.2	58.9	66
Hong Kong SAR	0.3	-10.0	29.7	91.2	246.8
Iceland	79.9	-7.3	49.7	35.3	189.5
Ireland	59.8	-5.3	28.7	44.1	72
Israel	73.0	-11.8	46.4	44.9	75.5
Italy	155.6	-9.5	57.3	65.3	115.6
Japan	256.2	-12.6	46.7	103.8	111.1
Korea	48.7	-2.8	25.6		
Latvia	45.5	-3.9	42.5		
Lithuania	47.0	-8.0	42.0		
Luxembourg	25.5	-3.8	47.5	70.8	342
Malta	55.4	-9.0	45.9		
The Netherlands	54.0	-5.6	46.9	104.6	152.2
New Zealand	41.3	-5.7	42.4	97.6	77
Norway	41.4	-7.0	58.2	114.9	155.2
Portugal	131.6	-6.1	48.1	68.3	103.4
Singapore	128.4	-8.9	26.6	55.4	140.8
Slovak Republic	60.7	-7.3	49.6		
Slovenia	81.5	-8.5	53.2		
Spain	117.1	-11.5	52.3	62.5	107.7
Sweden	38.5	-4.0	53.1	95.3	175.3
Switzerland	42.9	-2.6	36.3	132.7	137.5

Country					
Colombia	62.8	-6.9	33.4	32	34.7
Croatia	87.2	-8.0	55.0		
Ecuador	64.6	-6.3	36.9		
Egypt	90.2	-7.9	27.2	21	68.2
Hungary	81.2	-8.5	50.9	37.7	57.5
India	89.6	-12.3	31.0	17.8	22.6
Indonesia	36.6	-5.9	18.2		
Iran	42.8	-8.4	18.0		
Kazakhstan	27.4	-7.3	25.5		
Kuwait	11.5	-9.4	65.9		
Malaysia	67.5	-5.1	25.4	76.4	73.5
Mexico	60.6	-4.6	29.1	17.4	27.3
Morocco	76.1	-7.6	36.3		
Oman	81.1	-17.3	51.6		
Peru	35.4	-8.4	26.4		
Philippines	47.1	-5.5	25.1		
Poland	57.7	-8.2	48.9	34.9	45.6
Qatar	71.8	1.3	34.3		
Romania	50.1	-9.7	38.8		
Russia	19.3	-4.1	38.8		
Saudi Arabia	32.4	-11.1	40.3	22.1	93
South Africa	77.1	-12.2	40.1	14.6	61
Sri Lanka	100.1	-11.9	21.5	36.1	38.1

Annex Table (cont.)

Advanced countries	Gross public debt	Overall balance	Public expenditure	Household debt	Corporate debt
	2020	2020	2020	2020	2020
United Kingdom	103.7	−13.4	50.3	90.0	79.9
United States	127.1	−15.8	46.2	79.5	84.6

Emerging economies	Gross public debt	Overall balance	Public expenditure	Household debt	Corporate debt
	2020	2020	2020	2020	2020
Thailand	49.6	−4.7	25.3	77.8	53.4
Turkey	36.8	−5.4	34.6	17.5	72.1
Ukraine	60.7	−6.2	47.1		
United Arab Emirates	38.3	−7.4	32.0		
Uruguay	66.3	−4.9	33.3		

Source: IMF

Bibliography

Abiad, A., Detragiache, E. and Tressel, T. (2010). A New Database of Financial Reforms. *IMF Staff Papers*, 57(2), 281–302.

Acharya, V. V., Pedersen, L. H., Philippon, T. and Richardson, M. (2017). Measuring Systemic Risk. *Review of Financial Studies*, 30(1), 2–47.

Adalet McGowan, M., Andrews, D. and Millot, V. (2017). The Walking Dead? Zombie Firms and Productivity Performance in OECD Countries. OECD Economics Department Working Papers, No. 1372. Paris: OECD Publishing.

Afonso, A., Schuknecht, L. and Tanzi, V. (2005). Public Sector Efficiency: An International Comparison. *Public Choice*, 123, 321–47.

Afonso, A. and Schuknecht, L. (2019). How 'Big' Should Government Be? EconPol Working Paper 23/2019.

Aghion, P. and Mhammedi, A. (2021). The Keys to Inclusive Growth. *Project Syndicate*, 25 November. www.project-syndicate.org/commentary/inclusive-growth-competition-policy-and-flexicurity-by-philippe-aghion-and-aymann-mhammedi-2021-11.

Agnello, L. and Schuknecht, L. (2011). Booms and Busts in Housing Markets: Determinants and Implications. *Journal of Housing Economics*, 20(3), 171–90. https://doi.org/10.1016/j.jhe.2011.04.001.

Aizenman, J. and Marion, N. (2011). Using Inflation to Erode the US Public Debt. *Journal of Macroeconomics*, 33(4), 524–41.

Akgun, O., Bartolini, D. and Cournède, B. (2017). The Capacity of Governments to Raise Taxes. OECD Economics Department Working Papers 1407.

Alesina, A. and Ardagna, S. (2010). Large Changes in Fiscal Policy: Taxes versus Spending. *Tax Policy and the Economy*, 24, 235–68.
(2013). The Design of Fiscal Adjustments. *Tax Policy and the Economy*, 27, 19–68.

Alesina, A., Favero, C. and Giavazzi, F. (2019). *Austerity: When It Works and When It Doesn't*. Princeton, NJ: Princeton University Press.

Arnold, T., Gulati, M. and Panizza, U. (2020). How to Restructure Euro Area Sovereign Debt in the Era of Covid–19. *Capital Markets Law Journal*, 15(3), 322–46.

Arslan, Y., Drehmann, M. and Hofmann, B. (2020). Central Bank Bond Purchases in Emerging Market Economies. Bank for International Settlements (BIS) Bulletin No. 20.

Banerjee, R. N. and Hofmann, B. (2020). Corporate Zombies: Anatomy and Life Cycle. BIS Working Paper 882.

Bank for International Settlements (BIS) (2018). *Annual Report*. Basel: BIS.

Blanchard, O. (2019). Public Debt and Low Interest Rates. Peterson Institute of International Economics Working Paper 19-4.

Bordo, M. D. and Levy, M. D. (2021). Do Enlarged Fiscal Deficits Cause Inflation: The Historical Record. *Economic Affairs*, 41(1), 59–83.

Borio, C. and Disyatat, P. (2011). Global Imbalances and the Financial Crisis: Link or No Link? BIS Working Paper 346.

Borio, C., Contreras, J. and Zampoli, F. (2020). Assessing the Fiscal Implications of Banking Crisis. BIS Working Paper 893.

Borio, C., Disyatat, P., Juselius, M. and Rungcharoenkitkul, P. (2017). Why So Low for So Long? A Long Term View of Real Interest Rates. BIS Working Paper 685.

Borio, C., Lombardi, M. and Zampoli, F. (2016). Fiscal Sustainability and the Financial Cycle. BIS Working Paper 552.

Brunnermeier, M. (2021). *The Resilient Society*. Princeton, NJ: Princeton University Press.

Çelik, S., Demirtaş, G. and Isaksson, M. (2019). Corporate Bond Markets in a Time of Unconventional Monetary Policy. OECD Capital Market Series, Paris.

Checherita-Westphal, C., Hallett, A. H. and Rother, P. (2014). Fiscal Sustainability Using Growth-Maximising Debt Targets. *Applied Economics*, 46(6), 638–47.

Codogno, L. and van den Noord, P. (2020). Going Fiscal? A Stylised Model With Fiscal Capacity and a Eurobond in the Eurozone. Amsterdam Centre for European Studies Research Paper No. 2020/03.

Codogno, L. and van den Noord, P. (2021). Assessing Next Generation EU. LEQS paper No.166/2020, February. www.lse.ac.uk/european-institute/ Assets/Documents/LEQS-Discussion-Papers/LEQSPaper166.pdf.

De Larosière, J. (2019). Nous sommes entrés dans une ère ou la dette dirige nos économies. *Les Echos*, 22 June.

Detken, C. and Smets, F. (2004). Asset Price Booms and Monetary Policy. In H. Siebert (ed.), *Macroeconomic Policies in the World Economy*. Berlin: Springer, pp. 189–232.

Deutsche Bundesbank (2018). *Finanzstabilitätsbericht* [Financial Stability Report]. Frankfurt: Deutsche Bundesbank.

(2019). *Finanzstabilitätsbericht* [Financial Stability Report]. Frankfurt: Deutsche Bundesbank.

(2021). Government Finances: Central Bank Bond Purchases Increase the Sensitivity to Interest Rate Changes. Monthly Report, June.

Diessner, S. and Lisi, G. (2021). Masters of the 'Masters of the Universe'? Monetary, Fiscal and Financial Dominance in the Eurozone. *Socio-Economic Review*, 18(2), 313–35.

Dow, C. (2013). *Inside the Bank of England: Memoirs of Christopher Dow, Chief Economist 1973–84*. Houndmills, Basingstoke: Palgrave Macmillan.

Eichengreen, B. (2016). The Global Monetary Order. In *The Future of the International Monetary and Financial Architecture*. Frankfurt: European Central Bank, pp. 21–63.

Eichengreen, B., Mehl, A. and Chiţu, L. (2017). *How Global Currencies Work*. Princeton, NJ: Princeton University Press.

Eichengreen, B., El-Ganainy, A.,Esteves, R. and Mitchener, K. J. (2021). *In Defense of Public Debt*. Oxford: Oxford University Press.

Eren, E., Schrimpf, A. and Sushko, V. (2020). US Dollar Funding Markets during the Covid-19 Crisis: The Money Market Fund Turmoil. Bank for International Settlements (BIS) Bulletin 14.

Erhard, L. (1957/2009). *Wohlstand für Alle*. Köln: Anaconda. Published in English as *Prosperity for All*. New York: Frederik Plaeger.

Eschenbach, F. and Schuknecht, L. (2004). Budgetary Risks from Real Estate and Stock Markets. *Economic Policy*, 19(39), 313–46. https://doi.org/10 .1111/j.1468-0327.2004.00125.x.

Espitia, A., Mattoo, A., Rocha, N., Ruta, M. and Winkler, D. (2021). Pandemic Trade: COVID-19, Remote Work and Global Value Chains. *World Economy*. https://doi.org/10.1111/twec.13117.

European Banking Authority (2016). *Annual Report*. Luxembourg: Publications Office of the European Union.

European Central Bank (ECB) (2010). The 'Great Inflation': Lessons for Monetary Policy. *European Central Bank Monthly Bulletin*, May.

(2021). *Financial Stability Review*. Frankfurt: ECB.

European Commission (2018). Ageing Report: Economic and Budgetary Projections. European Commission Institutional Paper 079, Brussels.

(2020). The 2021 Ageing Report: Underlying Assumptions and Projection Methodologies. Institutional Paper 142, Brussels.

(2021). Debt Sustainability Monitor 2020. Institutional Paper 143, Brussels.

European Fiscal Board (2020). *Annual Report 2020*. Brussels: European Fiscal Board.

Federal Reserve Bank of New York (2021). *Center for Microeconomic Data*. www .newyorkfed.org/microeconomics/sce/labor#/expectations-job-search16.

Feld, L., Jungen, P. and Schuknecht, L. (2021). Why the Social Market Economy Succeeds. *Project Syndicate Long Reads*, March.

Feldstein, M. (2013). An Interview with Paul Volcker. *Journal of Economic Perspectives*, 27(4), 105–20.

Fuest, C. and Gros, D. (2019). Government Debt in Times of Low Interest Rates: The Case of Europe. EconPol Europe Policy Brief 16/2019.

G20 (2020). Common Framework for Debt Treatments beyond the DSSI. Saudi Arabia: G20 Finance Ministers and Central Bank Governors Meeting.

Goodhart, C. and Pradhan, M. (2020). *The Great Demographic Reversal: Ageing Societies, Waning Inequality, and an Inflation Revival*. London: Palgrave Macmillan.

Gründler, K. and Potrafke, N. (2020). Fiscal Rules: Historical, Modern, and Sub-national Growth Effects. CESifo Working Paper 8305.

Hank, R. (2012). *Die Pleiterepublik: Wie der Schuldenstaat uns entmündigt und wie wir uns befreien können* [The Bankrupt Republic]. Munich: Blessing Verlag.

Hartmann, P. and Smets, F. (2018). The European Central Bank's Monetary Policy during Its First 20 Years. *Brookings Papers on Economic Activity*, 2018(2), 1–146.

Hauptmeier, S., Heipertz, M. and Schuknecht, L. (2007). Expenditure Reform in Industrialised Countries: A Case-Study Approach. *Fiscal Studies*, 28(3), 293–343.

Hauptmeier, S., Sanchez-Fuentes, A. J. and Schuknecht, L. (2011). Towards Expenditure Rules and Fiscal Sanity in the Euro Area. *Journal of Policy Modelling*, 33(4), 597–617.

Havlik, A., Heinemann, F., Helbig, S. and Nover, J. (2021). Dispelling the Shadow of Fiscal Dominance? Fiscal and Monetary Announcement Effects for Euro Area Sovereign Spreads in the Corona Pandemic. ZEW Discussion Papers No. 21-050.

Heinemann, F. (2021). The Political Economy of Euro Area Sovereign Debt Restructuring. *Constitutional Political Economy*, 32, 502–22.

Heinemann, F., Moessinger, M. D. and Yeter, M. (2018). Do Fiscal Rules Constrain Fiscal Policy? A Meta-Regression-Analysis. *European Journal of Political Economy*, 51, 69–92.

Hilscher, J., Raviv, A. and Reis, R. (2014). Inflating Away the Public Debt? An Empirical Assessment. NBER Working Paper 20339.

Hofmann, B., Shim, I. and Shin, H. S. (2020). Emerging Market Economy Exchange Rates and Local Currency Bond Markets amid the Covid-19 Pandemic. BIS Bulletin No. 5.

Homer, S. and Sylla, R. E. (1991). *A History of Interest Rates*. New Brunswick, NJ: Rutgers University Press.

Institute of International Finance (IIF) (2021a). *Global Debt Monitor*, February. (2021b). Supply Chain Disruptions Continue to Build. *Global Macro Views*, 10 June. (2021c). The US Yield Conundrum. *Global Macro Views*, 17 June.

International Monetary Fund (IMF) (2018). *Global Financial Stability Report (GFSR)*. Washington, DC.

(2020a). *Global Financial Stability Report (GFSR)*, October. Washington, DC.

(2020b). The International Architecture for Resolving Sovereign Debt Involving Private-Sector Creditors – Recent Developments, Challenges, And Reform Options. Policy Paper No. 2020/043.

(2020c). *Fiscal Monitor*, October. Washington, DC.

(2021a). *Fiscal Monitor*, April. Washington, DC.

(2021b). *Fiscal Monitor*, October. Washington, DC.

(2021c). *Global Financial Stability Report (GFSR)*, April. Washington, DC.

(2021d). *Global Financial Stability Report (GFSR)*, October. Washington, DC.

(2021e). Review of the Debt Sustainability Framework for Market Access Countries. Policy Paper No. 2021/003.

(2021f). *World Economic Outlook (WEO)*, April. Washington, DC.

(2021g). *World Economic Outlook (WEO)*, October. Washington, DC.

Issing, O. (2021). The Return of Inflation? *Project Syndicate*, 16 July.

Jaeger, A. and Schuknecht, L. (2007). Boom-Bust Phases in Asset Prices and Fiscal Policy. *Journal of Emerging Markets Finance and Trade*, 43(6), 45–66.

James, H. (2021). The Janus of Debt. *Project Syndicate*, 8 October.

Jonung, L., Kiander, J. and Vartia, P. (eds.) (2009). *The Great Financial Crisis in Finland and Sweden: The Nordic Experience of Financial Liberalization*. Cheltenham, UK: Edward Elgar.

Jonung, L., Schuknecht, L. and Tujula, M. (2009). The Boom–Bust Cycle in Finland and Sweden 1984–95 in an International Perspective. In L. Jonung, J. Kiander and P. Var (eds.), *The Crisis of the 1990s in Finland and Sweden: The Nordic Experience of Financial Liberalization*. Cheltenham, UK: Edward Elgar.

Kelton, S. (2020). *The Deficit Myth: Modern Monetary Theory and the Birth of the People's Economy*. New York: Public Affairs.

Kreditanstalt für Wiederaufbau (KfW) (2020). *Kommunalpanel 2020*. Frankfurt: KfW.

Klöckers, H. and Mehl, A. (2021). The International Role of the Euro. European Central Bank, OMFIF Webinar.

König, N. and Schuknecht, L. (2019). The Role of Government and Trust in the Market Economy. CESifo Working Papers 6997. In W. Heusel and J. P. Rageade (eds.), *The Authority of EU Law – Do We Still Believe in It?* New York: Springer.

Kornai, J. (1986). The Soft Budget Constraint. *Kyklos*, 39, 3–30.

Krause, M. U. and Moyen, S. (2016). Public Debt and Changing Inflation Targets. *American Economic Journal: Macroeconomics*, 8(4), 142–76.

Krugman, P. (2020). Interview in L. Jacobson, Here Is Why Top Economists Are Not Worried about the National Debt, *CNBC*.

Laeven, L. A. and F. V. Valencia (2008) Systemic Banking Crises: A New Database. IMF Working Paper 08/224: 1–78.

Lee, K. Y. (1998). Asia in Crisis: Risk and Chances. Speech to the Dusseldorf Industry Club, 8 October. www.nas.gov.sg/archivesonline/data/pdfdoc/1998100803.htm.

MacKenzie, J. (2013). In Visit with Pope, Angela Merkel Urges Strong Financial Regulation. *Christian Science Monitor*, 18 May. www.csmonitor.com/World/Latest-News-Wires/2013/0518/In-visit-with-Pope-Angela-Merkel-urges-strong-financial-regulation.

Mayer, T. and Schnabl, G. (2021). How to Escape from the Debt Trap: Lessons from the Past. Flossback von Storch Research Institute.

Mitchener, K. J. and Trebesch, C. (2021). Sovereign Debt in the 21st Century: Looking Backward, Looking Forward. National Bureau of Economic Research Working Paper No. 28598.

Norimasa, Y., Ueda, K. and Watanabe, T. (2021). Emerging Economies' Vulnerability to Changes in Capital Flows: The Role of Global and Local Factors. Bank of Japan 21-E-5.

North, D. C. and Weingast, B. R. (1989). Constitutions and Commitment: The Evolution of Institutions Governing Public Choice in Seventeenth-Century England. *The Journal of Economic History*, 49(4), 803-32. https://doi.org/10.1017/S0022050700009451.

OECD (2015). *Results of the OECD-CoR Consultation of Subnational Governments*. Paris: OECD Publishing.

(2019a). *Budgeting and Public Expenditures in OECD Countries 2019*. Paris: OECD Publishing.

(2019b). *Budgeting Outlook*. Paris: OECD Publishing.

(2020a). *Taxing Wages 2020*. Paris: OECD Publishing.

(2020b). *Shocks, Risks and Global Value Chains: Insights from the OECD METRO Model*. Paris: OECD Publishing. Trade and Agriculture Policy Brief. https://issuu.com/oecd.publishing/docs/metro-gvc-final.

(2021a). *Assessing the Economic Impacts of Environmental Policies*. Paris: OECD Publishing.

(2021b). *OECD Economic Outlook*, 2021(1). Paris: OECD Publishing.

Official Monetary and Financial Institutions Forum (OMFIF) (2021). *Global Public Investor 2021.* www.omfif.org/wp-content/uploads/2021/07/GPI-2021.pdf.

Papaconstantinou, G. (2016). *Game Over.* Kyriakos Papadopoulos Publishing.

Rajan, R. and Zingales, L. (2003/2018). *Saving Capitalism from the Capitalists.* India: HarperCollins.

Reinhart, C. and Rogoff, K. (2009). *This Time is Different: Eight Centuries of Financial Folly.* Princeton, NJ: Princeton University Press.

Reinhart, C. M. and Rogoff, K. S. (2010). Growth in a Time of Debt. *The American Economic Review,* 100(2), 573–78. https://doi.org/10.1257/aer.100.2.573.

Reinhart, C. M. and Sbrancia, M. B. (2015). The Liquidation of Government Debt. *Economic Policy,* 30(82), 291–333.

Roos, J. E. (2019). *Why Not Default? The Political Economy of Sovereign Debt.* Princeton, NJ: Princeton University Press.

Ruiz Rivadeneira, A. M. and Schuknecht, L. (2019). Ensuring Effective Governance of Public Private Partnerships, *Journal of Infrastructure Policy and Development,* 3(2). https://doi.org/10.24294/jipd.v3i2.1148.

Schrimpf, A., Shin, H. S. and Sushko, V. (2020). Leverage and Margin Spirals in Fixed Income Markets during the Covid-19 Crisis. *BIS* Bulletin No. 2.

Schuknecht, L. (2018). The Supply of Safe Assets and Fiscal Policy. *Intereconomics,* 53(2), 94–100.

(2020a). *Preparing for the Recovery: More Market, Better Government.* London: Politeia.

(2020b). *Public Spending and the Role of the State.* Cambridge: Cambridge University Press.

Schuknecht, L., Moutot, P., Rother, P. and Stark, J. (2011). The Stability and Growth Pact: Crisis and Reform. *European Central Bank Occasional Paper* 129.

Schuknecht, L. and Tanzi, V. (2005). *Reforming Public Spending: Great Gain, Little Pain.* London: Politeia.

Schuknecht, L. and Zemanek, H. (2020). Public Expenditures and the Risk of Social Dominance. *Public Choice,* 188(1–2), 95–120. https://doi.org/10.1007/s11127-020-00814-5.

Schwartz, G., Fouad, M., Hansen, T. and Verdier, G. (2020). *Well Spent: How Strong Infrastructure Governance Can End Waste in Public Investment.* Washington, DC: International Monetary Fund.

Sinn, H. W. (2014). *The Euro Trap.* Oxford: Oxford University Press.

Stark, J. (2021). Jetzt haben wir sie bald – die Schulden- und Haftungsunion [It is coming, the debt and liability union]. *Welt,* 15 March 2021.

Summers, L. (2021). Opinion: The Biden Stimulus Is Admirably Ambitious. But It Brings Some Big Risks, Too. *The Washington Post*, 4 February 2021.

Tanzi, V. (2016). Pleasant Dreams or Nightmares in the Public Debts Scenarios? International Scientific Symposium and Official Ceremony to mark Hans-Werner Sinn's Retirement and the 25th Anniversary of the Center for Economic Studies (CES), University of Munich, 22 January 2016. www .cesifo.org/DocDL/sd-2016-09-tanzi-abschied-sinn-2016-05-12.pdf.

(2018). The Irresistible Attraction of Public Debt. In R. Wagner (2020) *James M. Buchanan: A Theorist of Political Economy and Social Philosophy.* London: Macmillan, ch. 43.

Tanzi, V. and Schuknecht, L. (2000). *Public Spending in the 20th Century: A Global Perspective*. Cambridge: Cambridge University Press.

Vissing Jorgensen, A. (2020). The Treasury Market in Spring 2020 and the Response of the Federal Reserve. Manuscript, University of California, Berkeley.

Volcker, P. A., and Harper, C. (2018). *Keeping At It: The Quest for Sound Money and Good Government*. New York: Public Affairs.

Wissenschaftlicher Beirat beim BMWi (2020). *Öffentliche Investitionen in Deutschland: Probleme und Reformbedarf* [Public investment in Germany: problems and reform needs]. Berlin: BMWi.

Wong, C. (2021). *Plus ça change: Three Decades of Fiscal Policy and Central-Local Relations in China*. Singapore: East Asian Institute.

Zettelmeyer, J., Trebesch, C. and Gulati, M. (2013). The Greek Debt Restructuring: An Autopsy. *Economic Policy*, 28(75), 513–63.

Zettelmeyer, J. (2020). Sovereign Debt Workouts: Developments, Challenges and Reform Options. *Mimeo*.

Acknowledgements

This study was produced while I was a visiting professor at the Lee Kuan Yew School of Public Policy. I am very grateful for comments from and discussions with Adrien Bussy, Lorenzo Codogno, Bert Hofman, Boris Hofmann, Lars Jonung, Danny Quah, Ramkishen Rajan, Kenneth Reinert, Juergen Stark, Vito Tanzi, Karsten Wendorf, Jeromin Zettelmeyer, Huanhuan Zheng and especially Jan Kallmorgen. I also thank the participants of the NUS/Lee Kuan Yew School of Public Policy and OMFIF panel on debt sustainability, the participants of the East Asian Institute research seminar in Singapore and two anonymous referees for their comments and suggestions. I am grateful to Bhavya Gupta for valuable research assistance, for which financial support from the Lee Kuan Yew School of Public Policy is thankfully acknowledged. The views expressed here are my own, and all remaining errors are my responsibility.

I dedicate this study to my parents who inspired my passion
for adventure, learning and research.

Cambridge Elements

International Economics

Kenneth Reinert
George Mason University

Kenneth A. Reinert is Professor of Public Policy in the Schar School of Policy and Government at George Mason University where he directs the Global Commerce and Policy master's degree program. He is author of *An Introduction to International Economics: New Perspectives on the World Economy* with Cambridge University Press and coauthor of *Globalization for Development: Meeting New Challenges* with Oxford University Press. He is also editor of *The Handbook of Globalisation and Development* with Edward Elgar and co-editor of the two-volume *Princeton Encyclopedia of the World Economy* with Princeton University Press.

About the Series

International economics is a distinct field with both fundamental theoretical insights and increasing empirical and policy relevance. The *Cambridge Elements in International Economics* showcases this field, covering the subfields of international trade, international money and finance, and international production, and featuring both established researchers and new contributors from all parts of the world. It aims for a level of theoretical discourse slightly above that of the *Journal of Economic Perspectives* to maintain accessibility. It extends Cambridge University Press' established reputation in international economics into the new, digital format of *Cambridge Elements*. It attempts to fill the niche once occupied by the *Princeton Essays in International Finance*, a series that no longer exists.

There is a great deal of important work that takes place in international economics that is set out in highly theoretical and mathematical terms. This new Elements does not eschew this work but seeks a broader audience that includes academic economists and researchers, including those working in international organizations, such as the World Bank, the International Monetary Fund, and the Organization for Economic Cooperation and Development.

Cambridge Elements ≡

International Economics

Elements in the Series

Debt Sustainability: A Global Challenge
Ludger Schuknecht